BETWEEN
HOME ᴬᴺᴰ_ᵀᴴᴱ FRONT

BETWEEN HOME AND THE FRONT

CIVIL WAR LETTERS *of the* WALTERS FAMILY

EDITED BY
LYNN HEIDELBAUGH
and THOMAS J. PAONE

SMITHSONIAN NATIONAL POSTAL MUSEUM
WASHINGTON, DC
IN ASSOCIATION WITH
INDIANA UNIVERSITY PRESS

This book is a publication of

Indiana University Press
Office of Scholarly Publishing
Herman B Wells Library 350
1320 East 10th Street
Bloomington, Indiana 47405 USA

iupress.org

Manufactured in the United States of America

First printing 2022

Library of Congress Cataloging-in-Publication Data

Names: Heidelbaugh, Lynn, compiler. | Paone, Thomas J. (Thomas
    John), compiler. | National Postal Museum (U.S.), compiler.
Title: Between home and the front : Civil War letters of the Walters family /
    [compiled by] Lynn Heidelbaugh, and Thomas J. Paone.
Other titles: Civil War letters of the Walters family
Description: Bloomington : Indiana University Press, [2022] | "Smithsonian
    National Postal Museum Washington, DC, In association with Indiana
    University Press." | Includes bibliographical references and index.
Identifiers: LCCN 2022000158 (print) | LCCN 2022000159 (ebook) | ISBN 9780253062963
    (hardback) | ISBN 9780253062970 (paperback) | ISBN 9780253062987 (ebook)
Subjects: LCSH: Walters, David W., 1838?-1865—Correspondence. | Walters, Rachel Ward, 1842?-—
    Correspondence. | Walters, Isaac, 1832-1917—Correspondence. | United States. Army. Indiana
    Cavalry Regiment, 5th (1862-1865) | United States. Army. Indiana Infantry Regiment, 20th (1861-
    1865) | Walter family. | United States—History—Civil War, 1861-1865—Personal narratives. |
    Indiana—History—Civil War, 1861-1865—Personal narratives. | United States—History—Civil
    War, 1861-1865—Regimental histories. | Indiana—History—Civil War, 1861-1865—Regimental
    histories. | Soldiers—United States—Biography. | Brothers—United States—Biography.
Classification: LCC E601 H45 2022 (print) | LCC E601 (ebook) | DDC 973.7/81—dc23/eng/20220408
LC record available at https://lccn.loc.gov/2022000158
LC ebook record available at https://lccn.loc.gov/2022000159

Cover credits: Detail of print: Thomas Nast, *Christmas Eve* (published *Harper's Weekly*, January
3, 1863). Detail of letter: National Postal Museum, Smithsonian Institution, 1991.0291.109.

CONTENTS

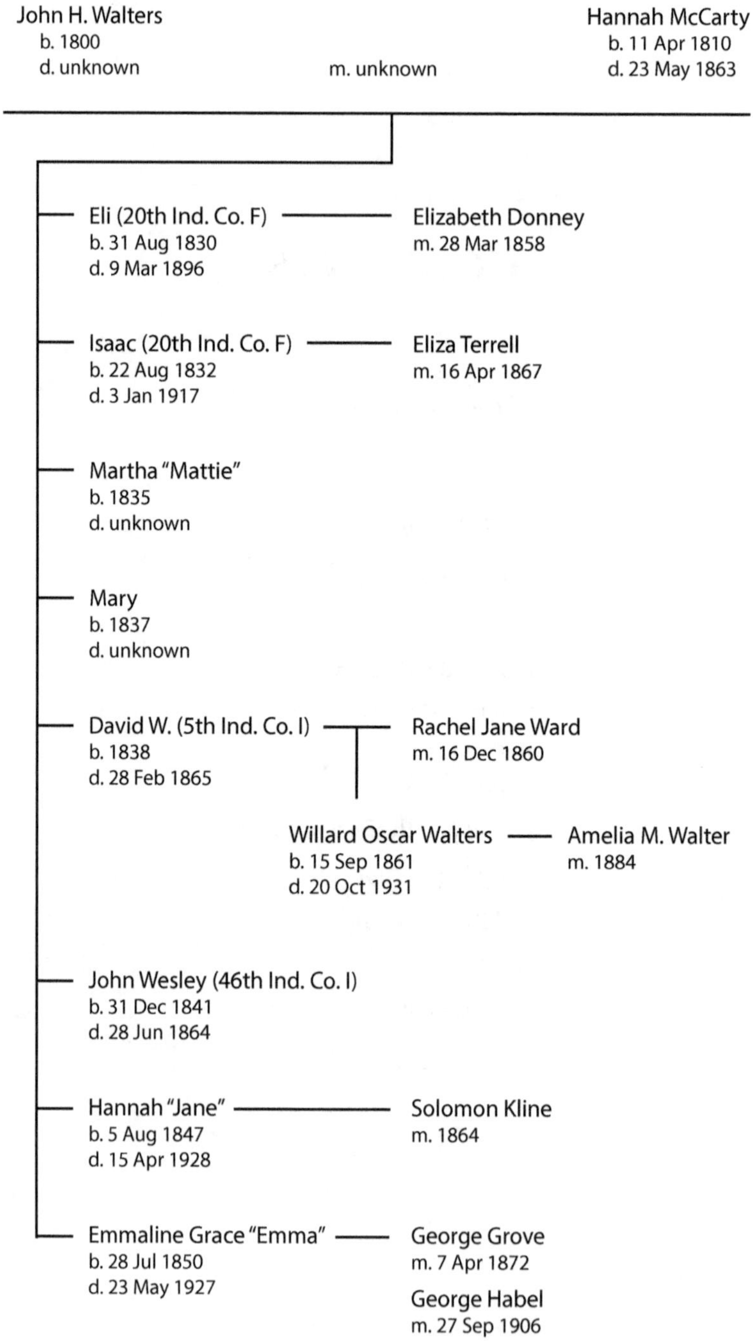

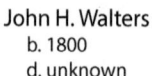

John H. Walters
b. 1800
d. unknown

m. unknown

Hannah McCarty
b. 11 Apr 1810
d. 23 May 1863

Eli (20th Ind. Co. F) ———— Elizabeth Donney
b. 31 Aug 1830   m. 28 Mar 1858
d. 9 Mar 1896

Isaac (20th Ind. Co. F) ———— Eliza Terrell
b. 22 Aug 1832   m. 16 Apr 1867
d. 3 Jan 1917

Martha "Mattie"
b. 1835
d. unknown

Mary
b. 1837
d. unknown

David W. (5th Ind. Co. I) ——— Rachel Jane Ward
b. 1838   m. 16 Dec 1860
d. 28 Feb 1865

Willard Oscar Walters ——— Amelia M. Walter
b. 15 Sep 1861   m. 1884
d. 20 Oct 1931

John Wesley (46th Ind. Co. I)
b. 31 Dec 1841
d. 28 Jun 1864

Hannah "Jane" ———————— Solomon Kline
b. 5 Aug 1847   m. 1864
d. 15 Apr 1928

Emmaline Grace "Emma" ——— George Grove
b. 28 Jul 1850   m. 7 Apr 1872
d. 23 May 1927
                                            George Habel
                                            m. 27 Sep 1906

Walters family tree. (*Graphic by Ashley Hornish*)

Samuel Ward, Jr.
b. about 1819
d. before 1880

m. 22 Mar 1840

Sarah Ann Fallis
b. 25 May 1820
d. 21 Dec 1905

Rachel Jane ——————— David W. Walters (5th Ind. Co. I)
b. 1842   m. 16 Dec 1860
d. 15 Dec 1868

Phebe A. ——————— Isaac Dunkin (20th Ind. Co. D)
b. 1843   m. 6 Mar 1863 (d. 24 Apr 1863)
d. unknown
                                 Wm. H. Johnston (7th Ohio Co. M)
                                 m. 4 Jul 1866 (d. unknown)

                                 [unknown first name] Gardner
                                 m. before 1898

Arthur M. ——————— Nancy E. Vaughn
b. Jun 1846   m. 8 Jun 1875
d. unknown

William Edwin "Eddy" ——— Helena McKinney
b. 7 Oct 1849   m. 2 Apr 1900
d. 27 May 1913

Mary J.
b. Apr 1850
d. unknown

Adam John ——————— Martha E. Cason
b. 21 Feb 1852   m. 25 Mar 1874
d. 6 Apr 1934

Sarah L. ——————— William Willis
b. 1853   m. 21 Jul 1875
d. unknown

Milo Presley ——————— Joy Wier Newman
b. 1856   m. 1 Jun 1881
d. unknown

Emma E. ——————— George W. Wright
b. 25 Sep 1857   m. 31 May 1877
d. 19 Apr 1882

Morris S. ——————— Emma A. McNabb
b. 25 Feb 1865   m. 11 Mar 1886
d. 18 Feb 1953

Ward family tree. (*Graphic by Ashley Hornish*)

Origins of letters for Rachel and David Walters, 1859–1866. (*Map by Kellee Koenig*)

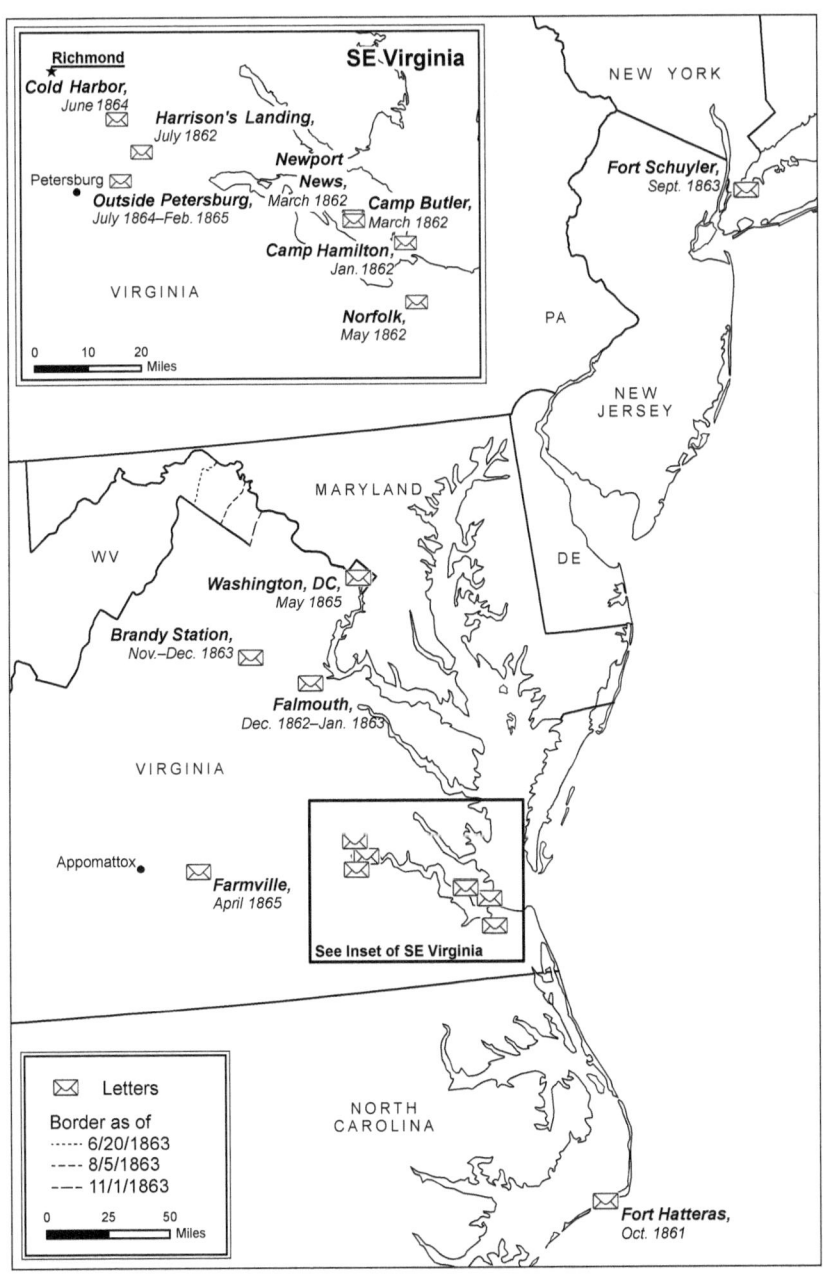

Origins of letters from Isaac Walters, 1861–1865. (*Map by Kellee Koenig*)

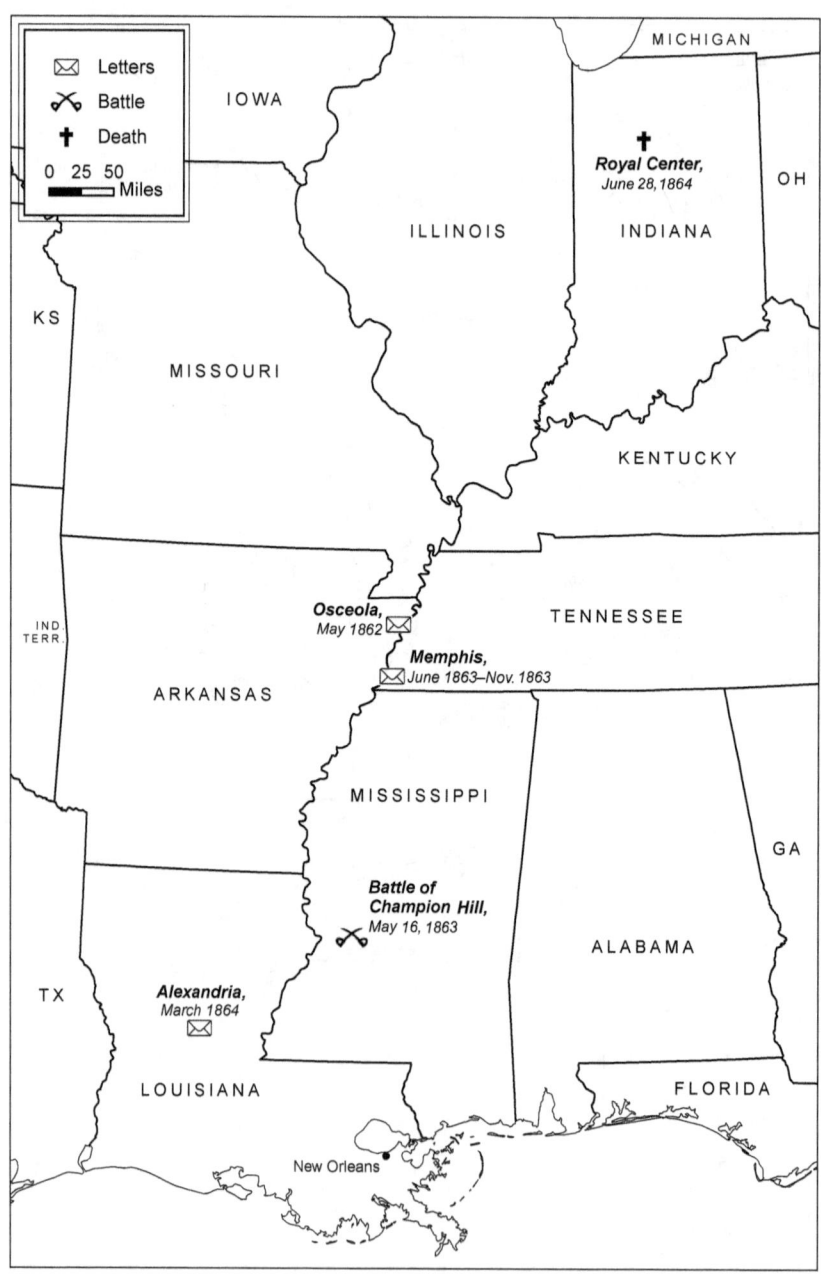

Origins of letters from John Wesley Walters, 1862–1864. (*Map by Kellee Koenig*)

ACKNOWLEDGMENTS

WE WOULD LIKE TO OFFER special thanks to several people whose talents enriched this work and made the book project possible.

Ashley Hornish transformed genealogical information into two family trees for this book, helping us all to see the many lives and relationships impacted by the American Civil War. Kellee Koenig designed maps to help plot out where the letters originated from to show the world of Rachel Walters and the vast swaths of the United States covered by three soldiers who called central Indiana home. Amanda Paone provided an excellent index, allowing researchers to better search this material and open it up to a broader audience, as well as incredible support throughout the project. Judith Heidelbaugh assisted with proofreading and advice.

Julie Flake provided crucial genealogical research that helped identify members of both the Ward and Walters families and solved several mysteries that arose from the breadcrumbs of information found in the letters. Rev. Albert H. Ledoux, PhD, and John L. Andrews Jr. of the Friends of Florence Stockade shared invaluable information regarding David's time as a prisoner of war. Terry Reimer of the National Civil War Medicine Museum discussed Clara Barton's Missing Soldiers Office and offered insight into how Rachel Walters interacted with this office.

Anna Francis, Ashley Runyon, and the staff of Indiana University Press provided essential guidance through the editing process and helped create a book that was far better than anything we could have imagined. Two anonymous readers provided corrections, recommendations, and constructive comments to improve our interpretive essays and editorial notes. Their insights were invaluable. Any inaccuracies or errors that remain are ours alone.

Numerous staff around the Smithsonian Institution made the dream of this publication a reality, including Laura Eichorn with the Smithsonian's Office of Contracting and Nicholas Partridge with the National Air and Space Museum, who provided critical assistance in shepherding this project from a vision to a publication contract; Katherine Krile with the Smithsonian Institution Traveling Exhibition Services; Mallory Warner with the National Museum of American History; Baasil Wilder with the Smithsonian Libraries and Archives; and our colleagues at the National Air and Space Museum and the National Postal Museum, with special thanks for the advice of Daniel Piazza and Susan Smith, and assistance on this project provided by Polone Bazile, Toby Cain, Ren Cooper, Scott Devine, Elizabeth Heydt, Manda Kowalczyk, William Lommel, Nancy Pope, Patricia Raynor, and the many other members of the National Postal Museum staff who have helped with this publication project and maintained this collection.

Most importantly, we owe a debt of gratitude to the descendants of the Walters family, who preserved these letters through the generations and entrusted them to the National Postal Museum, Smithsonian Institution. We wish to thank June Leonard, Cynthia Crank, and Emily Duffelmeyer for their offers of assistance. Without the family's collective sacrifice, foresight, and understanding of the importance of the written word, this incredible story would have been lost to the ages.

ABOUT THE LETTERS

READING AND WRITING LETTERS CAN build and sustain significant psychological and social connections for individuals, families, and communities. During the American Civil War, Rachel, David, and Isaac Walters—the primary letter writers in the Walters Family collection at the Smithsonian's National Postal Museum—along with their families and friends put pen to paper, recorded their messages in a specific moment and for specific audiences, turned to familiar phrases as well as formal epistolary customs, and relied on the mail to maintain their relationships. The documents in the collection provide personal perspectives on historic events. The letters saved by Rachel Walters and protected by her descendants offer remarkable insights into the impact of the war on the lives of individuals. Some of the letters reference others sent and received for which there are no corresponding documents in the collection. In some instances, the mail may not have been delivered and received, but more likely it either did not come back into the possession of Rachel Walters or was misplaced over the years.

The Walters family's correspondence collection came to the Smithsonian Institution by way of a letter from June Leonard on behalf of her father, Arthur W. Walters, grandson of Rachel and David Walters. Mrs. Leonard contacted the National Museum in the autumn of 1964, offering to donate Civil War and nineteenth-century documents. From the family's papers, the Smithsonian curators selected several items, including seven religious tracts and a temperance society certificate that became part of the museum's Division of Political History; a medical furlough issued to David Walters that went to the Division of Medical Sciences; and seven envelopes with patriotic decorations and addressed to Mrs. Rachel J. Walters that became part of the Division of Philately's collection. The bulk of the correspondence remained with the family until 1991, when staff of the Division of Philately, already working to create the National Postal Museum, contacted Mrs. Leonard to express interest in the other letters, envelopes, and documents of her grandfather, Willard, and great-grandparents, Rachel and David Walters. The resulting gift included 179 items, which, united with the seven previously donated envelopes, became part of the collection of the newly formed National Postal Museum that opened two years later.[1]

Over the years, the museum has exhibited portions of this collection for public engagement and access. The annotated transcriptions in this book are part of the museum's effort to preserve and make the material available to researchers. We transcribed the letters to be as true as possible to the original documents; the spelling, grammar, and punctuation, or lack thereof, are retained, but the traditional editorial notation [*sic*] is not used to denote deviations from modern American English standards because the differences in language use in these texts are too numerous. By not correcting or modernizing these elements, we intended to reflect the style and language of the individual writers. Many of the texts do not contain periods at the end of sentences; instead the writers frequently used extra spaces, which have been replicated. Strikethroughs represent words crossed out by the letter writers. Altogether the correspondence reveals variations in literacy levels and backgrounds in common oral traditions of the writers. Indeed, reading mail aloud was a common practice when sharing the news with family and neighbors. Reading the transcriptions aloud may bring clarity to some of the spelling and punctuation variations.

We did, however, adapt the formatting for publication, including the layout of the date and place of the letter's writing, salutation, valediction, and postscript. Brackets in the transcriptions indicate attributions or editorial notations, including the addition of full names of individuals deduced from the context of the documents, illegible words and phrases, portions of text that are differently oriented on the original page, or where the writing material changed in the document, such as inks.

The addition of notes throughout the transcriptions is intended to provide contextual information and clarification of proper names and place-names. We described the stationery to give a sense of the look and feel of the material used by the writers and held by the readers. These descriptions appear together with notations of information contained on available matching envelopes. This includes postage charges and changes of address that affected the sending and receipt of the mail. The postmarks that indicated where and when the items entered the postal network helped us complete the chronology and mapping of the letters. Information regarding the thirty envelopes in the collection that do not have matching letters is not included in this publication. We also did not include transcriptions of nine letters that did not further our understanding of the lives and history of the Walters family in the postwar period.[2] We provided the National Postal Museum's accession numbers to assist future research into this collection of letters, envelopes, documents, and associated ephemera.[3]

NOTES

1. Mrs. Robert M. Leonard to US National Museum, September 4, 1964; US National Museum Accession Memorandum, November 20, 1964, Accession file 0.256400, National Postal Museum, Smithsonian Institution, Washington, DC; National Museum of American History Accession Memorandum, n.d.; Joseph Geraci to Collections Committee, April 3, 1991, Accession file 1991.0291, National Postal Museum, Smithsonian Institution, Washington, DC.

2. Eight letters, dating between May 28, 1865, and September 6, 1868, were sent to Rachel Walters from friends and family: Nellie Washby (1991.0291.129), Lu E. Moore (1991.0291.116, 1991.0291.118, 1991.0291.114, 1991.0291.120), Maggie J. Porter (1991.0291.122), Arthur M. Ward (1991.0291.124), and Susanna Ballinger (1991.0291.126). A ninth letter dated June 25, 1880, written by Samuel Wall (1991.0291.137) was likely sent to Willard O. Walters and included a blank pension form for "Application of Children for Additional Bounty, Act, July 28, 1866" (1991.0291.138). The collection also includes three other documents that we did not transcribe: Willard O. Walter's pension certificate for minor heir, date stamped 1873 (1991.0291.136), incomplete pension form for "Children with Two Dollars per Month Additional" (1991.0291.139), and a leaflet (1991.0291.141) of "A Patriotic Speech by an Illinois Farmer," which was delivered by Senator Isaac Funk (1797–1865) to the Illinois legislature in 1863.

3. All citations with the accession numbers beginning with 0.256400 and 1991.0291 reference items in the collection of the National Postal Museum, Smithsonian Institution.

BETWEEN
HOME AND THE FRONT

As of July 1861, postal regulations permitted envelopes endorsed "soldier's letter" along with the signature of a commanding officer to be sent without prepayment of postage. Rachel J. Walters had to pay the three cents due to collect this mail sent by her husband, David, from Glasgow, Kentucky, in June 1863. A matching letter has not been identified. (*National Postal Museum, Smithsonian Institution, 0.256400.6*)

ONE

INTRODUCTION

I now take up my pen to write you a few lines to let you know
that I have not forgotten you.

—Rachel J. Ward to David W. Walters, July 28, 1859

RACHEL'S INVITATION TO DAVID

Eighteen-year-old Rachel J. Ward expressed her emotional attachment to a
twenty-year-old man in the next county by writing to him in 1859, "I expected
certain to see you last sunday and felt very much disappointed by not seeing
you   I feel very bad and do not expect to feel any better until I do see you."
David W. Walters of Cass County should have received Rachel's invitation to
a summertime picnic in Pulaski County in time to attend the social gathering
set for two days after Rachel wrote the message. She left little doubt about her
hopes—"I want to see you very much and cannot be satisfied without seeing
you"—and she may have entrusted the note to be hand-delivered by a friend.
Alternatively, she may have brought it to the post office, but no matching envelope postmarked with dates or locations is known to exist to provide evidence
that it traveled through the mail. In fact, it may never be known if Rachel sent it
or if David received it. However, the sentiments and paper remain, passed down
by the descendants of Rachel and David, who eventually wed on December 16,
1860. Just four days after the couple married, the United States began to fracture
when the state of South Carolina seceded. As events began to pull their nation
apart, the Walterses relied on letters to fortify their marital and familial bonds
during the American Civil War. The collection of their letters encompasses
several people in the young couple's social and emotional worlds and spans
time from a moment in their courtship to the aftermath of the national conflict.

Rachel J. Ward to David W. Walters

July the 28th 1859
Mooresburg Pulaski Co Ind

My dearest friend

I now take up my pen to write you a few lines to let you know that I have not forgotten you   the time seems long since I last saw you   I expected certain to see you last sunday and felt very much disappointed by not seeing you   I feel very bad and do not expect to feel any better until I do see you

we are going to have a picnic on next saturday which is the 30th of July and you are especialy infited[1] as many as can come and I shall be very happy to see you here   I am well at this time ~~ex prest~~ excepting a very bad cold   I want to see you very much and cannot be satisfied without seeing you but I must come to a close as I have nothing to interesting to write and not much time either   please excuse all mistakes and write soon and let me know how you are so no more at present

from your most dear and affectionate friend
Rachel J Ward

to
David W Walters[2]

when this you see
remember me[3]

THEIR FAMILIES

Rachel (Ward) Walters and David Walters shared similar backgrounds. Both of their families came to northwestern Indiana from Ohio between the late 1830s and 1850s. They were part of successive waves of white settlers arriving after people of the Potawatomi nation were forcibly removed from land ceded to the United States in the 1832 Treaty of Tippecanoe.[4] The families lived by Christian beliefs, worked farms, and sent their children to school, where they learned to read and write.

The Ward Family

Records for Rachel's family in Indiana began with her father, Samuel Ward Jr., who made a homestead in Pulaski County in 1839. The 1883 publication *Counties of White and Pulaski, Indiana* named Samuel as one of the first "pioneers" who "came from Ohio, or some of the Eastern States, and commenced the construction of their new homes in the then wild and distant West." There he purchased 160 acres in the newly established Harrison Township in 1841. He ran for office the same year and was active in the township, which was notable in the county's history for being "solidly Republican on all State and National questions" between the 1840 and 1880 elections. Furthermore, he held a very public job as appointed postmaster of Mooresburg between 1853 and 1862.[5]

Along with the growth of his civic engagements, Samuel's domestic responsibilities multiplied too. He married Sarah Ann Fallis, a fellow Ohioan whose family had also emigrated to Indiana. Sarah gave birth to their first child, Rachel, around 1842. Rachel grew up with four sisters and five brothers, and the siblings' world became larger still when they went to school. Rudimentary education included lessons in reading and writing, and Rachel may have had further opportunities to develop penmanship and to study composition and etiquette for letters. A similar curriculum would have been taught at the school that David Walters attended while growing up in Fulton County, Ohio. The time available for studying and school, however, depended on demands for labor on the family farm.[6] Moreover, Rachel and her eldest siblings would have witnessed, and possibly assisted with, their father's postal duties. Post offices in a community the size of Mooresburg did not typically produce much profit but could bring in extra income while requiring relatively few hours to run the simple operations out of the postmaster's residence or place of business.[7] Samuel would have overseen the accounts, sorted the incoming and outgoing mail, and visited with the customers coming to buy stamps and pick up their letters and newspapers. News of the day could be overheard as the neighbors came and went on their errands at the post office, giving the Ward household an opportunity to engage in discourse outside their family.

The Walters Family

Like the Ward family, John and Hannah (McCarty) Walters had lived in Ohio. The couple, originally from Pennsylvania, had four boys and four girls between 1830 and 1850. Sometime after the 1850 census was taken, members of the Walters family relocated from Ohio to northern Indiana, perhaps motivated by opportunities to purchase farmland or work as agricultural laborers. The war further uprooted the family, and eventually the four Walters brothers—Eli, Isaac, David, and John Wesley—would leave Cass County, Indiana, to volunteer for the Union army.

The Walters brothers had each signed enlistment papers by August 1862. In contrast, the sons in the Ward family were too young for soldiering, but their father, Samuel Ward Jr., found at least one way to support the Union cause and served as an enrollment official for Pulaski County.[8] Despite the state's diverse political climate, the residents of Indiana showed fervor for the Union's cause in the early months. Politicians and civic leaders gave impassioned speeches both in the Indiana State House and in communities throughout the state to encourage support for the Union and the war effort by enlisting in the military or providing for those who did.[9] Indiana quickly met the federal government's quota to raise six infantry regiments. In fact, by the end of 1861, Indiana had raised fifty regiments for service, or approximately fifty thousand men.[10] The volunteerism that swayed the men who answered the call in 1861 and 1862 built the militaries of both the Union and Confederacy.[11]

Patriotic sentiments and desire to serve echoed in several of David's letters, and on September 29, 1862, he wrote to Rachel, "I feel that our contry needs my help & I am willing to do all that I can & eaven give my life for your libertys & our beloved childs." In his very next letter to Rachel on October 1, 1862, David repeated the explanation of his motivation to volunteer, telling Rachel that he was sorry "that you ar put to so much trouble with our things but it cant be helped now & I feel that I am doing my duty in helping to maintain the laws of our country & put down this wicked rebellion." Men who volunteered in the Union and Confederate armies exhibited similar ideas about honor and duty; moreover, regardless of social and economic factors, many believed they could not stay home while other men went off to fight.[12] Whatever the reason, each of the four Walters brothers found themselves committing to the Union army, and they, like other soldiers, faced competing priorities when reenlistment time came. In contrast to the early waves of patriotic-driven volunteerism, the soldiers who joined after the first waves were often swayed by financial incentives, such as signing bonuses known as bounties, or because they were drafted into the military after the government introduced conscription as the number of voluntary enlistments began to fail to meet the manpower needs of the armies depleted by years of warfare.[13]

Although Isaac Walters quickly joined the Union war effort, he did so without the moral and financial obligation of a dependent wife or family. By contrast, his brothers Eli and David were both married at the time they volunteered almost a year later. Married farmers grappled with how going off to war might put their families and farms at risk of economic ruin.[14] James McPherson explained, "Married soldiers confronted a dilemma caused by competing ideals of manhood and honor. In one direction lay their responsibilities as husbands, fathers, and breadwinners for dependents to whom they had made a sacred pledge to cherish and support. In the other direction lay their duty as able-bodied citizens to defend their country. To evade either obligation would dishonor their manhood. But in time of extreme national peril, the manly call of duty to country seemed more urgent."[15] Such concerns affected the composition of regiments recruited in the area. As Thomas E. Rodgers pointed out, "Of the married men [in the west-central area of Indiana], only 25.5 percent served in the military at any time during the conflict, while 51.6 percent of the single males served. . . . Not only did relatively few married men serve, but many of those who did were at home for most of the war."[16] The fact that David served at all is quite remarkable given the demographics in his region of the state. The twenty-three-dollar bounty quoted in his letter of September 6, 1862, could have partly motivated his volunteering and brought solace that what he was to receive for signing up would help provide for his family. The burdens caused by David's absence as a husband and father and competing obligations to family and nation featured throughout the Walterses' wartime correspondence.

HOOSIERS AND THEIR RESPONSES TO THE WAR

Although the voluntary enlistment of the Walters brothers demonstrates how they supported the Union, similar commitment to the war effort cannot be attributed to all residents of Indiana or other states in the North. The election of 1860 saw Republican Oliver P. Morton, a vocal proponent of Abraham Lincoln and a strong supporter of the Union war effort, leading a politically divided state.[17] The outbreak of the war briefly brought most of Indiana's Republicans and Democrats together, as support for the common cause of preserving the Union had wide appeal across the political parties.[18] By 1862, however, multiple crises throughout the nation and Union military defeats ended this temporary unity in Indiana.

President Abraham Lincoln issued the Emancipation Proclamation in September 1862, an act that alienated Democrats who had supported the war as a way to preserve the Union but not as a war for emancipation. Setbacks on the battlefields further compounded dissension among some northern Democrats, who became known as Peace, or antiwar, Democrats. A growing opposition to the war won the Democrats a majority in both houses of the Indiana legislature in the October 1862 elections, leaving the state government split. The Peace Democrats vocally opposed the Republican governor Oliver P. Morton as he backed President Lincoln and managed to ensure that the state fulfilled quotas for regiments and readied supplies for them.[19] As the deadlock between Governor Morton and the Peace Democrats continued into 1863, Morton took the extraordinary step of working around the legislature regarding the state budget. Republicans refused to meet in a session of the legislature, so a quorum could not be established, and then Morton simply refused to call the legislature back into session.[20] Morton effectively ran the state alone for twenty-two months, ignoring the legislature's demands, and Peace Democrats continued to protest throughout the state for the duration of the war, causing great tension throughout cities and small communities.[21]

The draft, authorized by the United States Congress in March 1863, further enflamed political hostilities that led to violent actions. The new law angered Peace Democrats because it had the potential to force men who did not support the war to join the military. Resistance to the draft was common in Indiana, and the discord could turn violent.[22] In a letter dated June 23, 1863, Rachel Walters recalled an incident surrounding a local effort to draft soldiers. She wrote to her husband, "I believe I told you in another letter that they was enrolling the men for another draft   there is so many secesh in fulton Co that some of them refused to be drafted enrolled and they beat one of the enrolling officers almost to death and burned all his papers so the Gov sent on a lot of soldiers to take care of them." Clearly, the military conflict and political affairs shaped lives and colored the worldview of every American. Although the correspondents of the Ward and Walters families tended not to delve deeply into accounts of battles or wartime politics, as will be seen, the events permeated the thoughts, opinions, and practical quotidian concerns they shared by mail.

THE WALTERS BROTHERS ON THE MILITARY FRONT

The military lives of Isaac, David, and John Wesley Walters mirrored the regional and national levels of strife, as is evident in the letters they each wrote to Rachel, David's wife.[23] Isaac's enlistment with the Twentieth Indiana Infantry Regiment took him to the Eastern Theater of the war, starting off the coast of North Carolina and proceeding to numerous battles in Virginia. During the summer of 1862, Isaac and the Twentieth Indiana participated in the Peninsula Campaign, fighting in the Battles of Yorktown, Glendale, and Malvern Hill, among others. Isaac continued to serve in the Twentieth Indiana through some of the fiercest battles of 1862 and 1863, including the Battles of Fredericksburg, Chancellorsville, and Gettysburg. The Twentieth Indiana engaged in the Overland Campaign in 1864, fighting battle after battle with the Army of Northern Virginia, including the Battles of the Wilderness, Spotsylvania Courthouse, and Cold Harbor. By the end of the year, Isaac's regiment besieged the city of Petersburg, Virginia, during which he wrote frequently while moving camp and engaging Confederate forces as his unit edged closer to Richmond. The year 1865 saw the fall of Petersburg and Richmond, after which the Twentieth Indiana participated in the final pursuit and capture of the Army of Northern Virginia at Appomattox Court House. Through it all, Isaac endured illness, hours of guard duty, and many of the war's most infamous battles from the autumn of 1861 to the war's end in the spring of 1865.[24]

David Walters chose to serve in the cavalry, a branch of military service that was mounted on horseback, and joined the Fifth Indiana Cavalry Regiment. David's regiment deployed in 1863 to Kentucky to keep order in the border state and skirmished with local forces that were aligned with the Confederacy. One of the most notable campaigns of David's military career involved his unit's participation in dispatching Morgan's Raid. Brigadier General John Hunt Morgan, a Confederate cavalry commander, had ridden and raided with his troops through Kentucky and Tennessee throughout 1862. In July 1863, Morgan and 2,500 men under his command rode from Tennessee, through Kentucky, and eventually into Indiana, provoking fear among the populace of the state. Union commanders quickly mobilized the cavalry, including David's regiment, to meet the invasion. Morgan and his men caused damage throughout the areas they rode, but Union forces eventually captured the raiders by the end of July 1863.[25] David and his unit continued to serve in Kentucky and Tennessee through the spring of 1864, when they joined General William Tecumseh Sherman's campaign to capture Atlanta, Georgia. It would be David's final campaign of the war.[26]

His brother John Wesley Walters sent letters from points along the Mississippi River while serving with the Forty-Sixth Indiana Infantry Regiment in the Western Theater of combat. John Wesley participated in the attack on Island No. 10, as Union forces began to take control of the Mississippi River, a vital route for transporting supplies and troops as well as dividing the states aligned with the Confederacy. As the Union army moved deeper into the South, John Wesley and his regiment served in the army of Ulysses S. Grant. They took part in the Battle of Champion Hill, a critical engagement that pushed Confederate forces into the city of Vicksburg, Mississippi. A grueling siege ensued at this strategic location, about which President Lincoln is attributed to have remarked, "See what a lot of land these fellows hold, of which Vicksburg is the key. . . . The war can never be brought to a close until that key is in our pocket. We can take all the northern ports of the Confederacy, and they can defy us from Vicksburg."[27] Although the Forty-Sixth Indiana went on to fight in the siege of Vicksburg, wounds received at Champion Hill kept John Wesley off the front lines while he recovered.[28]

Each brother had a unique story to tell, but what they told in their letters and how they told it did not just depend on the immediate circumstances they faced. Personal preferences and social norms during the Civil War determined the amount of information, topics covered, and tone set by a letter's author. For instance, Isaac noted that he chose not to describe recent skirmishes in his March 24, 1862, letter to David and Rachel and his January 6, 1863, letter to Rachel. The omission of details about the battles was Isaac's prerogative.[29] Neither Union nor Confederate military officials censored soldiers' mail. They censored only prisoner-of-war mail and controlled the exchange of mail between the warring sides. Thus, the vast majority of correspondence between civilians and military personnel on the same side of the conflict traveled through the postal network without censorship of the messages. The more pervasive mediating factor of gender relations influenced the content of Isaac's letters to his brother and to his sister-in-law. How women and men interacted and how they thought they *should* relate to one another affected what they wrote to one another.

RACHEL WALTERS ON THE HOME FRONT

Rachel Walters became the nexus of communication and epistolary confidant for her husband, David, and his brothers Isaac and John Wesley. Rachel received their letters and relayed their news to family and friends. In her April 6, 1864 letter, she extended the network to her sister Phebe (Ward) Dunkin and allowed her to add passages. Through everything, the foremost audience for Rachel's messages was David, her husband and the father of their son, Willard.

Rachel's descriptions of daily activities reflected and reinforced how she performed the domestic, family-oriented, and moral roles expected of a wife, mother, and woman in the nineteenth century.[30] She wrote to David with a loving wife's affection. She also wrote with concern and advice on living a Christian life and modeled churchgoing behavior. She documented care and love for their infant son, nursing Willard when he was ill and finding joy in the new songs and games he learned. When possible, she supported David with mementos like photographs and material goods to sustain him as she would have if he had been home. Although the war stretched boundaries of gender norms for women (particularly for those of the middle classes and elites) and their participation in public, political, and economic life, these changes appear not to have been experienced by Rachel Walters herself.[31] Rachel remained outside the political realm but heard and discussed the news of violence in the community over issues of the draft. She did not participate in the events, or at least she did not record such actions that would be contrary to the pervading expectations for women. She told David about the crops grown by the Ward and Walters families and about teaching school, but neither the economic state of the farms nor taking on a job were atypical for a rural, working-class, white woman.[32] Rachel's life and work on the home front also held to traditionally acceptable patriotic acts—namely, writing letters to boost the morale of soldiers. In this way she performed her domestic roles, ensuring the sense of home and family that her letters reported to her soldier husband.

Rachel held the day-to-day responsibility for Willard Walters, or Willy and Willie as he was often referred to in the correspondence. Willard was not quite one year old when his father left home after joining the Union army in late 1862. Children experienced similar separations from parents during the war; in fact, Rachel also had to be away from Willard for a period in 1864 while she taught school. Although children may not have been fully aware of the social or political reasoning behind the war, they directly felt the effects. Children in the North lacked products that were once generally available and felt the impact of the deaths of friends, neighbors, and loved ones. Children in the South also experienced such traumas, but many suffered through even more critical and prolonged shortages of essentials as the war continued over years.[33] These hardships are featured in letters sent by parents. Mothers hoped to demonstrate how they nurtured the family, and fathers hoped to read of home and their children so they could escape the drudgery and tragedies at the front. Mail also enabled military personnel to parent in absentia, as James Marten remarked, "Civil War fathers desperately sought to project their authority and love through the erratic mails, remaining fathers in function as well as in name."[34] David Walters often wrote with instructions, such as on September 6, 1862, when he requested,

"Rachel i want you to take good care of everthing spesly of wiley." Rachel included news about Willy in almost all her letters, such as on October 7, 1862, when she told of Willy being "fretful" as a result of teething. Sharing of even the smallest details and practical matters like these helped create bonds but could not fulfill the demands of hands-on care in family affairs.

Through her letters Rachel also undertook the duty of instilling Christian morality in her family. She and her correspondents often shared thanks to an Almighty God in phrases that reflected the centrality of faith in America during the Civil War era. Religious sentiments, often in opening salutations, buoyed the writers' and readers' beliefs, helping them endure and reconcile the hardships of separation and death. Participation in religious denominations, especially Christian, increased throughout the early nineteenth century, with the 1850s seeing large revivals.[35] As the nation descended into war, Americans on both sides of the conflict looked to religious teachings to gain a better understanding of and to find justification for what was happening. People saw their allegiance to the war effort through the lens of religion. George Rable explained, "Few churchgoers hesitated to hitch their faith to patriotism, and the pious sent off young men to war with remarkable unity and enthusiasm. For clergy and laity alike, the war became a holy crusade."[36] With her husband committed to his military duty for the country, Rachel expressed her concern that David live according to their faith even while far from home. One of Rachel's passages in her letter of June 14, 1863, has the twofold purpose to implore David "to live faithful" and to bring him solace, as she wrote, "I truly feel thankful to the god of heaven in that he has heard and answered my prayers and I hope that he will continue so to do   O David try in to live faithful and grow in grace and in the knowledge of the truth as it is christ Jesus our lord that we may meet our dear mother and friends.   friends thats gone before in a better world above for I believe that she is as an angel watching and waiting to meet us the banks of sweet deliverance where partings are known no more." Religion helped console those who experienced tragedy and death, including those of David's mother at home and the family's friends in the war. The belief in the afterlife and spiritual immortality enabled Americans to accept the carnage and death they faced on a scale never before seen in the nation.[37]

The survival of Rachel's letters across decades testifies to the value many people placed on remembering this tragic period through materials, messages, and memories. Some of Rachel's writings to her husband, David, came back into her possession, perhaps retrieved from her husband's tin case that John S. Louderback, a fellow member of David's regiment, informed Rachel about in his May 27, 1865, message. Two of Rachel's letters came back to her by other means: the Post Office Department returned the mail she sent to Louderback on April 26, 1866, and Clara Barton's Missing Soldiers Office reused Rachel's July 21, 1866, stationery to respond to her in October. Regardless of when and how she obtained her own letters, that they still exist demonstrates the exceptional care taken to safeguard them—first by the postal service and military delivering them, then by David in keeping and carrying them, and later by Rachel and the family in saving them. The mail that survives from women on the home front is less common than that sent to the home front from military service members, who faced the agonizing reality that they simply could not carry the missives they received while living, moving, and fighting in the war zone.[38] Although many soldiers wrote about cherishing the mail from home, they often chose not to keep the material, only holding it dear in their memories like they did their loved ones. Reasons to shed the papers varied by individual and circumstance. Paper weighed down knapsacks and lacked durability when exposed to the elements, like rain and snow. Physical integrity aside, the sensitivity of the information read by the wrong eyes—either friend or foe—caused some to burn their pages and entreat their correspondents to do the same.[39] Michael Nelson analyzed gendered motivations behind the disposal of letters and papers during wartime when soldiers let go of the physical and tangible links to home and normalcy in ritual preparation for battle; and Confederate women facing invasion sought to destroy papers and diaries to "consign all evidence of their private selves to the flames in order to inhabit the persona of normative femininity: apolitical, passive, and traditionally literate."[40] Constructs of appropriate activities of women and men and perceptions of their roles in private and public spheres influenced who wrote contemporary narratives, including letters and journals; who that literature was for; and whose documents were published, preserved, or archived.[41]

The number of Rachel Walters's letters is in almost equal proportion to her husband David's, and brother-in-law Isaac's; and together, the letters written by the three of them make up the majority of the correspondence in this collection at the Smithsonian. Far fewer documents from John Wesley Walters, Phebe (Ward) Dunkin, and other family members and friends remain.

THE US MAIL AS USED BY THE WALTERS FAMILY

The family network would not have been possible without the postal network. Most people in circumstances similar to the Walters and Ward families—on the same side in the Union cause—experienced wartime changes in *how* they sent mail through the United States Post Office Department. The separation of

A mail wagon of the US Army II Corps at Brandy Station, Virginia, 1864, was part of the communication network for the Union forces. The Post Office Department and the military coordinated logistics to carry important official communiques and personal letters. (*Library of Congress, LC-DIG-ppmsca-34235*)

families and friends during the war had more Americans writing letters than ever before, but letter writing had been on the rise following postal rate reforms starting in 1845 that began to make mail more affordable. The introduction of the postage stamp in 1847 put the onus on the sender to prepay the costs, and mail became easier to access. In 1856, the post office required the use of stamps on letter mail, and Americans paid a penalty if they did not prepay. The war upset supply and demand of commonplace goods, stamps included. On July 22, 1861, the US government waived prepayment of postage on mail marked "soldier's letter" and that had been countersigned by an officer. A congressional act on January 21, 1862, allowed personnel in the US Navy and Marine Corps to do likewise. The granting of this convenience meant military service members did not have to scrounge for stamps in order to send letters. Nevertheless, when able to do so, many used stamps rather than the "soldier's letter" frank, which financially burdened the recipient. Some enclosed stamps for their correspondents, as Rachel Walters often tried to do for her husband.

Correspondents fulfilling requests for stamps demonstrated how greatly they valued their mail and each other. Most of the Walters and Ward families' letters cost three cents to send because they weighed less than half an ounce and they did not travel far enough for the distance factors of the 1855 and 1861 rates to apply. None of the letters in the collection were charged at the lesser drop letter rate. Only a couple were sent in the period of the 1855 rate, which calculated postage by weight and an additional expense for letters traveling more than three thousand miles. The rate that came into effect in the spring of 1861 changed the distance factor from miles to an additional charge for crossing the Rocky Mountains, but the postage rate introduced in 1863 further simplified the formula, and weight alone determined the cost of mailing a letter. This meant that the weight of the envelopes and paper themselves were of great importance, and the stationery available during the period varied greatly.

The market ranged from fine laid paper to thin sheets, and manufacturers typically embossed their products with their companies' names, symbols, and, sometimes, statements of quality. They created envelopes and sheets with patriotic imagery, including the latest battle scenes or prominent political and military leaders. Makers of Union or Confederate patriotic stationery found consumers eager to demonstrate their allegiance. As the war progressed and the Union blockades effectively prevented commodities from reaching Confederate-held ports, civilians and military members throughout the Confederate states turned to reusing and repurposing paper for their personal letters. Scarcity also hit some Union soldiers, usually when they ran short of cash. Charitable organizations, like the US Sanitary Commission, gave stationery to soldiers.[42] The US Christian Commission provided paper and stamped envelopes to help military service members stay in contact with home as part of the organization's comfort and welfare initiatives in its mission of spiritual support for Union soldiers.[43] Supplies could also be purchased from sutlers, who had official authorization to follow regiments and act as purveyors of goods to troops, and, while they sold food and clothing to supplement rations and general issue uniforms, they also furnished comforts such as tobacco, medicine, stationery, pencils, pens, ink wells, and even field desks.[44] Soldiers who bought dried ink had to mix it with water, and the success of reconstituted ink can be seen in the flow of their writing. Rachel Walters frequently opted for blue ink, but the various colored inks available at the time on the home front were not always sold by the sutlers. In short, the materials of letter writing became part of the message, both through their appearance and through the effort and expense necessary to acquire them.

Whether with pen or pencil in hand, filling a blank page with one's news and views could be daunting. Lined paper helped guide unsteady hands, but for soldiers, the surfaces they found to write on could be improvised and unstable. When sick, wounded, or illiterate, military personnel and civilians alike found they needed help with their writing and asked friends, family members, or hospital aides to take dictation. The semiliterate and those lacking confidence in their composition and penmanship also sought out the assistance of scribes. With practice and reliance on customary phrases, many developed their writing and voice. The letters of David Walters exhibit changes in both the handwriting and style of expression. It may be possible that someone lent him a hand, but his missives also suggest that he picked up conventions, for instance, when he borrowed a phrase from his wife, Rachel, and copied the use of the "N.B." postscript in her April 18, 1864, letter in his response on April 26, 1864. Writers learned from each other and relied on the rhetoric, etiquette, and common practices of letter writing to converse "through the great medium of ink and paper."[45]

During the nineteenth century, few alternatives to pen, paper, and the mail existed for communicating over distance. The telegraph service primarily connected government, business, and news reporters requiring speed of transmission. For tangible goods weightier than a letter, people turned to express companies for shipping and traveling friends to carry items as a favor. Not until January 1864 did Congress allow the mailing of up to two pounds of clothing to enlisted men, which enabled families to send assistance and comfort. Food and clothing supplements from home could be vital to soldiers' physical well-being. Wives, mothers, sisters, and daughters transmitted products of their traditional domestic work of feeding, mending, sewing, knitting, and nursing.[46] Soon after mustering in, David Walters wrote to his wife, Rachel, to request supplies that would help with his soldiering: goggles for eye protection and a pair of mittens with one finger specially knitted to wear while using a rifle. The couple told one another of sending and receiving items that reinforced emotional bonds and memories—photographs, jewelry, clothing, and even a souvenir from combat. They sometimes deliberated how to spare and send each other money. Pay for soldiers, often delayed and for particularly prolonged periods while on a campaign, created difficulties for the men and the families they supported. Some people chose the risky practice of enclosing currency with letters. Civilians and soldiers did not have accessible means for sending funds securely until November 1, 1864, when the Post Office Department introduced the money order service.[47]

Customers desired reliability in their postal service. The system could be imperfect and unpredictable in wartime, but the correspondents themselves did not always write and respond in a timely fashion. External demands caused pauses in the middle of composing, and writers resumed at a later hour or day after being called away for military duty or domestic chores. At times they struggled for words but filled the page with apologies for the lack of something to say. Rachel Walters and her sister Phebe (Ward) Dunkin acknowledged that letters lacked the give-and-take of in-person conversations and characterized their epistolary work as dialogues conducted through "the silent language of the pen."[48] The silence caused by delayed, lost, or unfulfilled responses triggered dismay in the best of times and brought about feelings of apprehension during times of strife. To avoid confusion and call attention to a letter that may have gone astray, writers typically prefaced answers with reference to specific mail received.[49] Prompt replies allayed fears and showed respect. Yet, wartime conditions affected expectations about the timeliness of mail exchanges. Locating soldiers and moving mail to and from the field proved challenging. In recognition of the special circumstances of troops on the move, the Post Office Department, as of the act of July 24, 1861, allowed prepaid letters to soldiers to be forwarded without charge. Delays could occur at the many points along the distribution chain. The Post Office Department's special military postal-service agents brought mail to and picked it up from the headquarters of Union armies and oversaw that these postal exchanges took place when possible.[50] Regimental mail orderlies, typically with the rank of private, gathered letters from soldiers and officers, took them to headquarters for outgoing dispatch, and returned with incoming mail for distribution to the men expecting word from home. Troops on scouting or advance duties had to wait to return to command to retrieve their mail, as David Walters described in his April 17, 1864, letter. Military service members and civilians alike experienced anticipation and anxiety while waiting for the mail. The correspondents and Post Office Department created the personal and national networks essential for keeping the Union in contact.

NOTES

1. "Infited," which should be read as "invited," is transcribed as it appears in the original letter. Corrections have not been made for spelling, grammar, and punctuation, but layout has been standardized and explanatory notations added to the transcribed text in this collection.

2. The intended recipient's name was commonly included at the end of a letter if the salutation did not specify.

3. The letter (1991.0291.41) was written in blue ink on laid stationery embossed with a paper manufacturer's mark, "Superfine," above a shield emblem. A matching envelope has not been identified.

4. Campion, "Indian Removal and the Transformation," 32–62.

5. Goodspeed and Battey, *Counties of White and Pulaski, Indiana*, 548–557. Leon M. Gordon's "The Price of Isolation in Northern Indiana, 1830–1860" provides an analysis of the geography and development of eleven northern counties including the Wards' home county of Pulaski, where the population "increased from 561 settlers in 1840 to 5,711 by 1860" (page 154).

6. The first two schools in Harrison Township opened in 1848 and 1849 (Goodspeed and Battey, *Counties of White and Pulaski, Indiana*, 553), but there are no check marks for school attendance in the 1850 census for Rachel Ward, age eight; her sister Phebe, age seven; and three younger siblings (1850 US Census, Harrison, Pulaski County, Indiana, page 351b, dwelling 369, family 369, Samuel Ward; digital image, Ancestry.com, accessed May 11, 2021). The Free School Law of 1852 mandated at least three months of annual funding for common schools, and the removal of some financial concerns such as tuition helped increase enrollment as more parents were able to send their children to school. When the 1860 census was taken, Rachel and six of her eldest siblings had attended school that year (1860 US Census, Harrison, Pulaski County, Indiana, page 49, dwelling 344, family 343, Samuel Ward; digital image, Ancestry. com, accessed May 11, 2021). Several siblings of David Walters were older than the Ward children, and according to the 1850 census, they had been in school in Ohio. Eli, Isaac, Martha, Mary, David, and John Wesley Walters all received some schooling (1850 US Census, Pike, Fulton County, Ohio, page 296, dwelling 378, family 380, John Walters; digital image, Ancestry.com, accessed May 11, 2021).

7. Blevins, *Paper Trails*, 99–108.

8. Rachel J. Walters to David W. Walters, June 14, 1863, National Postal Museum, Smithsonian Institution, 1991.0291.48.

9. Nation and Towne, *Indiana's War*, 48–49.

10. Nation and Towne, *Indiana's War*, 44.

11. The volunteers had considerable influence on the course of the war, as summarized by James McPherson in *For Cause and Comrades*: "During its first

year all of those who enlisted and fought on one side or the other chose to do so. The same was true of most soldiers and sailors during the war's second year. Together these volunteers of 1861 and 1862 constituted the overwhelming majority of genuine fighting men during the war. Without their willing consent there would have been no Union and Confederate armies, no Civil War" (pages 15–16).

12. McPherson, *For Cause and Comrades*, 14–18.

13. McPherson, *For Cause and Comrades*, 8–9.

14. Rodgers, "Hoosier Women and the Civil War," 111.

15. McPherson, *For Cause and Comrades*, 134.

16. Rodgers, "Hoosier Women and the Civil War," 111.

17. The election of 1860 saw Oliver P. Morton voted in as lieutenant governor of Indiana, with Henry S. Lane as governor, as well as the Republicans controlling both houses of the Indiana state legislature. Following the election, however, Lane was selected by the Republican-controlled state legislature to fill a seat in the US Senate, leaving Morton as governor of the state as the country devolved into civil war (Fuller, *Oliver P. Morton*, 69–70).

18. Nation and Towne, *Indiana's War*, 43–45.

19. Nation and Towne, *Indiana's War*, 43–44, 125–126.

20. Nation and Towne, *Indiana's War*, 126–127.

21. Fuller, *Oliver P. Morton*, 131.

22. Fuller, *Oliver P. Morton*, 135–136.

23. Eli Walters, the eldest brother, received a medical discharge in December 1862, having served for four months. There are no known letters by or to him.

24. National Park Service, "Battle Unit Details, Union Indiana Volunteers, 20th Regiment, Indiana Infantry."

25. Nation and Towne, *Indiana's War*, 146–148.

26. National Park Service, "Battle Unit Details, Union Indiana Volunteers, 5th Regiment, Indiana Cavalry (90th Regiment, Indiana Volunteers)."

27. Ballard, *Vicksburg*, 24.

28. National Park Service, "Battle Unit Details, Union Indiana Volunteers, 46th Regiment, Indiana Infantry."

29. For a study of soldiers' personal choices in their correspondence, see Bui, "'I Feel Impelled to Write.'"

30. For a discussion of wartime perceptions of women's roles at different life stages, see Etcheson, "Women and the Family."

31. For analysis of changes in gender norms during the Civil War, see Attie, "Warwork and the Crisis of Domesticity"; Rodgers, "Hoosier Women and the Civil War," 105–128; and Whites, "The Civil War as a Crisis in Gender."

32. Giesberg, *Army at Home*, 17–44. In *Those Good Gertrudes*, Geraldine Clifford provides the statistic that "in 1859 men were 80% of Indiana's teachers; by 1864, only 58%" (page 65).

33. Marten, *The Children's Civil War*, 7. Children and adults in the South suffered from food shortages brought on by increasing prices and the US naval blockade of Confederate ports; shortages increased over the course of the war as both armies foraged for or destroyed crops as they crossed the countryside. Compared to the North, more children in the Confederate states experienced firsthand the numerous battles that raged across their family's land and homes, some of which were completely lost as a result of the warring armies.

34. Marten, *The Children's Civil War*, 70.

35. Faust, *This Republic of Suffering*, 172.

36. Rable, *God's Almost Chosen People*, 7.

37. Faust, *This Republic of Suffering*, 176.

38. While surveying Civil War letters collections in museums, archives, and publications, we found comparatively fewer letters by women than men, but correspondence by women in this period is available, such as Budge Weidman's study, "'Dear Husband, Please Come Home,'" of African American women's letters that were submitted to army officials when soldiers requested furloughs, and the documents subsequently became part of the men's military service records; and, *Wanted—Correspondence* by Nancy Rhoades and Lucy Bailey, which focuses on one family's collection of 168 letters sent by women responding to a soldier's advertised request for correspondence.

39. Bui, "'I Feel Impelled to Write,'" 171–180.

40. Nelson, "Writing during Wartime," 57–61.

41. Nelson, "Writing during Wartime," 66–68. Christopher Hager's *I Remain Yours* also considers the presence and absence of women's letters in histories and collections that started with the challenges of battlefield conditions and continued through archiving practices (pages 107–109).

42. Isaac Walters enclosed his letter of July 8, 1862 (National Postal Museum, Smithsonian Institution, 1991.0291.75) in a US Sanitary Commission envelope (National Postal Museum, Smithsonian Institution, 1991.0291.76) with a three-cent stamp.

43. An envelope (0.256400.7) in the National Postal Museum collection bears the US Christian Commission name printed in the upper left corner: "U.S. Christian Commission / SOLDIER'S LETTER," and the three-cent George Washington stamp is canceled in the upper right corner. The postmark location of Washington, DC, is where some of Isaac Walters's mail passed through while he was in the Eastern Theater. Although dated June 15, the year is not discernable. Isaac Walters's handwriting is evident in the address to "Mrs. R. J. Walters. / Star. City / Pulaski. Co / Ind." There is no known letter associated with this envelope.

44. Lord, *Civil War Sutlers*, 55.

45. Isaac Walters to David and Rachel Walters, March 24, 1862, National Postal Museum, Smithsonian Institution, 1991.0291.69. For studies of how letter

writers improved their style and composition over repeated practice during the war, see Bailey, "'So Pleasant to Be a School Maam,'" and Hager, *I Remain Yours*.

46. Rodgers, "Hoosier Women and the Civil War," 119; Whites, "Written on the Heart."

47. United States Postal Service, *The United States Postal Service*, 18.

48. Rachel J. Walters to David W. Walters, December 22, 1863, National Postal Museum, Smithsonian Institution, 1991.0291.53; Rachel J. Walters and Phebe A. (Ward) Dunkin to David W. Walters, April 6, 1864, National Postal Museum, Smithsonian Institution, 1991.0291.55.

49. Some correspondents tracked gaps by writing numbers on the letters they sent, but the Walters family did not.

50. The United States Post Office Department's *Annual Report* in 1898 includes the first assistant postmaster general's comparison of the 1898 military mail operations in the Spanish-American War to that of 1861–1865, and he promoted, unsurprisingly, the regularity of the contemporary service over that of "the crude but courageously and bravely executed" antecedent (pages 120–121). The 1898 *Annual Report* also contains a special section from which the comparative analysis was drawn using government records that discussed the work of Colonel A. H. Markland, who was a general superintendent of military mail during the Civil War (pages 216–225).

TWO

—〰—

1861–1862

Rachel i want you to take good care of everthing spesly of wiley
and ned and fido   learn fido to bite ever body that comes their
and lern willey to dance and box and stand on his head.

— David W. Walters to his wife, Rachel, September 6, 1862

THE DECADES OF TENSION BUILDING within the United States regarding
the question of slavery reached a breaking point following the election of President Abraham Lincoln in 1860. Although Lincoln never declared during the
campaign that he would outlaw slavery, the Republican Party platform included
halting the spread of slavery into newly organized territories, a position that met
with strong opposition in the Southern states.[1] On December 20, 1860, South
Carolina formally seceded from the Union. Ten additional Southern states followed over the subsequent months, and, together, the eleven states eventually
formed the Confederate States of America. In response to President Lincoln's
refusal to turn over Fort Sumter to this new entity, Confederate forces opened
fire on April 12, 1861, on the US-held fort, located in the harbor of Charleston,
South Carolina, marking the start of the Civil War. The fall of Fort Sumter led
President Lincoln to call initially for seventy-five thousand volunteers to help
quell the rebellion.

Response from Indiana's residents exceeded the state's first recruitment
quotas, and the first regiments were formed by late April 1861. Between 1861
and 1862, the four sons of John and Hannah Walters of Indiana volunteered
for military duty with the Union. The second-eldest of the Walters sons, Isaac,
became the first to answer the call. Isaac Walters stood at a height of five feet,
ten inches and had a dark complexion, dark hair, and gray eyes.[2] The unmarried
farmer was a month shy of his twenty-ninth birthday when he joined enlistees

"View of the Camp of the 20th Indiana Regiment, Also Fort Hatteras, and the Anchorage at Hatteras Inlet, NC, Taken from the Ramparts of Fort Clark," published in *Frank Leslie's Illustrated Newspaper*, November 9, 1861, shows the site that Isaac Walters described as a "very Sickly hole" in his October 17, 1861, letter. *(Courtesy of Thomas J. Paone)*

from Cass County in Company F of the Twentieth Indiana Infantry Regiment. The volunteers gathered at Lafayette, Indiana, about forty-five miles southwest of Isaac's home in Royal Center. The mustering in took place on July 22, 1861, as a military officer led the newly enrolled men in swearing the oath to remain loyal to the country, abide by orders from their officers, and uphold the duties assigned to them.[3]

The earliest letter in the collection by Isaac is dated October 17, 1861, when he wrote to his brother David and sister-in-law Rachel from Fort Hatteras, North Carolina. By early October his regiment had trained, served guard duties in Maryland, and had its first encounter with Confederate forces at the Chicamacomico Races, Cape Hatteras. His letter carried a bleak account of the illnesses suffered by the regiment—the heat and humidity of the Outer Banks exacerbated disease and dehydration among the poorly supplied troops—and he told of his own bout with a fever. He found some happiness upon receiving word from David and Rachel, and confessed that he was "a little Surprised" by the timing of his nephew Willard's birth. Life-changing events of the family members would fill the pages of their correspondence and keep them engaged in each other's lives throughout the war.

The next to join the Union army was John Wesley Walters. At almost twenty years old, and the youngest of the four Walters brothers to volunteer, John Wesley enlisted at Royal Center, Indiana, on November 20, 1861.[4] He signed on for three years with Company I, Forty-Sixth Indiana Infantry Regiment. The Forty-Sixth Indiana officially mustered into service on December 11, 1861, and quickly moved to take part in several of the early battles fought along the Mississippi River, control of which was prioritized by the Union command in the Western Theater. From late February to early April, the regiment took part in the successful campaign to capture Island No. 10 and enable Union gunboats to pass a strategic section of the Mississippi River. John Wesley wrote to David and Rachel Walters on May 16, 1862, while near Osceola, Arkansas, and recounted his part in the May 10 naval engagement at Plum Run Bend, Arkansas.

Later that summer, both the eldest and third-eldest Walters brothers, Eli and David, respectively, enrolled on August 15, 1862. Eli joined in Logansport, Indiana, enlisting in the same company as his brother Isaac.[5] Meanwhile, in Valparaiso, Indiana, David enlisted in Company I, Fifth Indiana Cavalry (Ninetieth Regiment).

David Walters was a farmer from Royal Center, Indiana, when he volunteered for military service. He was about twenty-three years old, with a height of five feet, ten inches, a dark complexion, dark hair, and brown eyes.[6] He was married and had a son who was almost a year old. The existing letters by his wife, Rachel, do not comment on David's enlistment; however, she expressed strong misgivings in November 12, 1862, regarding David possibly joining the regular army and concluded that conversation point imploring, "O David I beg of you not to join the regulars   I want you to come home so bad so that we can go to house keeping again."[7] Unlike volunteer regiments, enlisting with the "regulars," the professional, permanent army, obligated soldiers for the duration of the war. Voluntary service had limited terms, and David had signed on for a three-year period. David's decision to go to war did not sit well with Isaac, who wrote to Rachel on December 1, 1862, "I think he ought to Stayed at home by all means if I Should have been placed in his circumstances I would have Stayed at home. I think it would have been more credit to him to have taken care of his family than to have gone to the army - but every one to their own notion."

David's letter of September 29, 1862, shows concern for his family in his absence and his intention to send funds to support them. He received a bounty as the state of Indiana, like many others, tried to entice men to enlist by offering financial incentives. The monetary bonuses along with the promise of steady pay attracted some men, but in reality, these were often delayed. Under the Union army system, personnel received their funds from the paymaster, who traveled to regiments and ensured accurate distribution and thorough documentation of the transaction as each soldier signed the roll. An "allotment plan" elected by a service member directed funds to a designated person, such as a spouse or parent. However, the military frequently did not meet the obligations to pay and equip personnel in a timely or sufficient manner, which compounded the burdens on the service members' dependents struggling with the absence of wage-earners. Erratic payments, sometimes months late, caused strain on soldiers as they tried to purchase needed items not issued by the army as well as see to their families' livelihood.[8]

Rachel took care of business matters at home and for her husband. On November 12, 1862, she sent David a dollar, writing, "[I]t is all I have now   Charles has not paid me yet we have got the corn gathered." She continued with a list of men in her family and locals who "helped" with the crop. Rachel then switched her letter's topic, turning to her motherly, domestic world as she wrote of the neighbor's babies and her own son, Willard. The situations Rachel described are not unlike historian Judith Giesberg's finding of Northern women whose "letters suggest that women in rural communities were in constant motion, doubling up the work of caring for children with taking over work on the farm."[9] At home, farms and businesses had to be maintained and family members nurtured and fed. The need to negotiate the pervading social mores and realities of new demands for her labor changed Rachel's daily life. One such change came when Rachel moved. By late September 1862, she began calling for her mail at the Star City post office rather than Royal Center, where David had sent his first letters to her shortly after he departed to muster in and begin his military training. Rachel's world had changed in profound ways in the first years of the war, as had the lives of the enlisted Walters brothers.

The indoctrination into the Union army delineated the soldier's sense of his civilian and military selves. New duties and skills, along with uniforms and regulations, created soldiers out of men like the Walters brothers. Trainees practiced how to move as one unit during a process often referred to as drill, which included marching, maneuvering, and the proper way to load and fire their weapons. The enlistees became part of a company, consisting of about one hundred men at the start of the war. Several companies then combined to form a larger unit, the regiment, often referred to by their number and state, such as the Twentieth Indiana. These units trained together so they could perform actions cohesively during the heat of combat. During a campaign, the units marched several miles each day, set up new camps each night, and deployed pickets, or advanced guards, around the camps to monitor for enemy attacks.[10] The letters of Isaac, David, and John Wesley Walters are peppered with military terms and discussion of their tasks, equipment, and experiences in the Union army.

ISAAC WALTERS TO DAVID AND RACHEL WALTERS

Fort Hateras[11]
Oct the 17th
/ 61

Dear Brother & Sister

it is with pleasure & gratitude that I write to you in order to let you know that I am in the land & among the living although I am not well but I am geting better   I received your letter last Sunday & was very glad to hear from you & hear that you ware all well & doing well & I hope you will Still Continue to do so   I was a little Surprised to hear that you had an heir[12]   So soon but I hope he will live &do well in order that dave will have Some body to Sit up corn for him   I fancy his name very much   I believe it is the very name that I would have given him myself   I hope he will grow to be a fine large boy by the time i get to see him & I hope the time is not far distant when we Shall meet again & Strike glad hands once more on this Side of the grave   I long to See you all & Still hope I will See you all again. In the first place I had a Spell of the fever & I got it broke & then I got the neueralga[13] ~~very~~ very weak yet & it appears that I cant gain any strength but I hope I will come all right after a while

there is nearly half of our regiment taking medacine at the present time & there is Still more taking Sick[14]   this is a very Sickly hole & I hope we will get away from here before long when we was ordered here Col brown[15] Shook his head & Said we had the worst place in in the world & one of the officers that helped take the place affirmed what col brown Said & I have found his words true for it is the Sickliest place that I ever Saw in my life I believe I have no more to write at present but remain you affectionate Brother until Death

Write Soon yours in love
Isaac Walters[16]

Isaac Walters to David and Rachel Walters

Camp Hamilton[17]
Jan the 27th
/62

Dear Brother & Sister

   I embrace the present to let you know that I am well at present &
hope these few lines may find you all enjoying good health & a degree of
happiness   I reced your letter a few days ago & was very glad to hear from
you & hear that you was all well   I want you to Still continue to write to
me & dont neglect it as I always like to hear from home & I will try to answer
all your letters punctually   pleas remember this will you   Some of
our men was out on a scout one night last week & they captured a rebel &
brought him into camp   our Company was Standing picket guard when
they brought him in & they had to come right by our pickets[18] & I saw him
as they were coming in & I would have given fifty dollars to have [*illegible
deletion*] had one Shot at him with my riffle   fifty yds I think I could have
tickled him Some any how   The weather has changed very much Since
I last wrote to you   our Sunshine has turned into hail & rain & it is very
muddy & disagreeable geting about at this present time yesterday was a very
nice day but today it is cloudy again   nothing more of importance has
occured Since I last wrote to you   Virgil Weekes just wrote to me   I
received his letter to day he is well   he is in Summerset Ky   he Says
his Co & regt enjoys very good health   he also Says he or his regiment
had a little fight with the rebel pickets lately he said they killed 7 of the
rebels & wounded & took 3 prisoners   he Said we dedent lose a Single
man in the fray   this is about the way it is going where ever we have an
engagement with damned rascals   I suppose you have seen an account of
Gen Zolacoffers[19] death   he was killed in the late battle in Ky   he was
a dreaded enemy but he has gone to reap his reward &just So all the rebel
army will go   you will See it
   I have only received one letter from Wes[20] Since he enlisted   I have
not heared from martha[21] for Some time neither   if I had wes by the wool
I will bet I would make him write   rachel I want you to give these few
lines in print to mother[22]   Write Soon &give me all the news   No
more at present

I remain as ever your
Sincere Brother & friend
excuse all mistakes
Isaac Walters[23]

ISAAC WALTERS TO DAVID AND RACHEL WALTERS

Dear Brother & Sister

I now compose myself in order to answer your letter which I received Some time ago but have not had an opportunity to answer your letter before now   I have been very busy since I got your letter & you will have to excuse me for not writing Sooner   your letter found me well & I hope this may find you all enjoying good health & I hope you are happy

This regiment has moved from Camp Hamilton to Newport news a distance of Eight miles   we moved last friday & have been very busy fixing up our new quarters & making our Selves as comfortable as we possibly can   our quarters are not as nice as they were at Camp Hamilton but I think we can make them just as good as they were   this is more pleasant looking than our other Situation was. it is Said by the Soldiers that our pickets at this place & the rebel pickets Stand in full view of each other. none of our regiment have been on picket yet at this place so I have not Seen any of the rebel pickets yet but I would like to See them mighty well but I will have to wait a while

I received a letter from martha last friday   She was well. She sent her miniature[24] to me She had it taken in delta   She said Mary Jane Hanpton took her picture & it is very good & nicely done   mother used to know her well. her & martha is just the Same age   mary jane & me used to have some great times when we were young & I would like to See her   first rate   She used to be a pretty smart girl & I guess She has not forgotten it yet. I also received a letter from Aunt Weeks not long ago. they ware all well   it is raining here to day & it looks like if we ware going to have more wet weather but I am getting so used to it that I dont mind it much   I Generally try to do like they do in Spain &let it flicker

When you write again let me know how your little boy is geting along. I would like to see him very much   I have forgotten his name I hope he is doing fine

I Suppose you think Soldiering agrees with me first rate by the looks of my picture   I have no more to write at present So I will close   the boys are all well that came from that part

Write Soon

Yours with Love & respect
Isaac Walters[25]

ISAAC WALTERS TO DAVID AND RACHEL WALTERS

Camp ~~Hamilton~~ Butler,[26] March 24th /62

Dear &much Loved Brother & Sister

I once more find myself Seated in order to converse with you at this great distance through the great medium of ink & paper

Your letter came to hand yesterday which I read with joy it found me well & I hope this letter may find you all participating in the Same blessing

This is a most beatiful morning & every thing glows with more than ordinary life & brilliancz   This is the most pleasant place we have been Since we left the State of Ind   Everyone appears to be full of life & activity

I would be very happy to See you all once more. The time Seems long Since last we met but I trust that we may be So happy as to See each other face to face ere the vale of death our vision darkens   Sometimes I think I never will See you any more in this life but if this Should be our lot my prayer is that we may meet in a fairer region above where parting will be no more for ever perhaps you may think I have become a praying man but to my own Sorrow & Shame This is not So. If I under Stand prayer it is the hearts Sincere desire utetered or unexpressed   General Wool[27] has made a recquisition for Sixty thousand troops for this place & I understand they are landing every day at fortress monroe[28]   I understand there is twenty thousand there now   as Soon as the required force gets here we are going to make a move on Some point   but where I cant tell certain but I think the first step will be to take york town

Yesterday all the troops at this place passed in reveiw & was inspected by General mansfield[29]   General Mansfield told Col brown to Stand in reainess that when a movement was made we Should not be left behind & perhaps it may be Some time before you will hear from me again   General Mansfield Says he thinks when we pull Stakes again we will not Stop very Soon but continue to advance & fight when ever an opportunity presents it Self & I think he is right for the way things are working I think it will require Such a movement in order to accomplish the desired end & if this Should be the case I will have a very poor chance to write   but I Shall write when ever an opportunity offers its Self   I dont want you to quit writing for your

Isaac Walters's elegantly written letter to his brother David and sister-in-law Rachel on March 24, 1862, began with phrases commonly used in correspondence of the era but became increasingly personal toward the end, culminating in a prominently placed valediction, "Yours in Heart." *(National Postal Museum, Smithsonian Institution, 1991.0291.69)*

I believe I am through for the
for the present So I will
Come to a close by asking
an interest in all your prayers
Give my warmest love to all my
inquiring friends

Yours in Heart

Isaac Walters

To David & Rachel

letters will follow us where ever we go   just direct them to the 20th regt & they will follow us no difference where we are

I would like to give you an account of our battle here but cant do it this morning for I have not time to do it. if you want to see it See Elis letter or Cousin Jacob Walterses[30]   I gave both of them a Short Sketch of the fight   The boys are all well except richard Scott   I think he is taking the consumption[31]   if this proves to be tha case he will be discharged from the Service & Sent home   dick is a good Soldier & will be miss by us very much if this Should be the case

I believe I am through for the present So I will Come to a Close by asking an interest in all your prayers   Give my warmest love to all my inquiring friends

Yours in Heart
Isaac Walters

To David & Rachel[32]

JOHN WESLEY WALTERS TO DAVID AND RACHEL WALTERS

May the 16th 1862

Dear Brother

I take my pen in hand to let you know that I am in the land &
Among the living & I am still able to keep the forked down   I must
tell you that I received your kind letter some time ago & was glad to
here from you but I am sorrow to here that phebe[33] was so bad but I
hope when these few lines comes to hand they may find you all well and
all the connection   I expect your boy is got to be quite a man by
this time   now I must tell you that we are all still in arcansas near
ocela[34] about 5 miles from the rebels   last Saturday we attacked
them with our gun boats[35]   they fought about one hour   they
disabled 2 of our gun boats & we sunk 2 of theirs & disabled one more
of theirs   they wouldent of had any of ours it they hadent of had a
buting ram   they ran into our boat 3 times & the 3 times they put
one hole rite threw the bough of our boat our boats are all ready now
for action   the dam cecesh[36] retreated back to their wholes for
if they hadent to of done just as they did we would [illegible deletion]
cleaned them out in about one hour longer they say that we have
tourn down their fort by shelling them like the devel   we sent 2
companies out on a scout last nite & they brought 16 cecesh prisoners
in with them this morning they tell us that the war cant last long   it
is very warm here now   it uncomfortable wearm here at this
time   we have little black stallion drille every day but it is awful
wearm

No more at this t time
to Rachel & D Walters
by J W Walters

Direct as before
Good by

[*Valediction continues at the top of the page.*]
but not Forever
J.W.W May the 16 1862[37]

Isaac Walters to David and Rachel Walters

Norfolk
May the 18th/ 62

Dear Brother &Sister

your kind letter Came to hand Several days ago & found me
well &I hope these few lines may find you all enjoying the Same
blessing   you must excuse me for not writing Sooner as we was on a
march when I received your letter & this is the first opportunity I have
had of answering your letter   We are encamped about one mile
from Norfolk   we with two other regiments & a company of cavalry
was ordered to march on to Norfolk the cavalry in the advance & when
the rebels Saw our cavalry approaching they fled without firing a gun
& our forces marched into the city with out any resistance & the mayor
of the city Surrendered the city to our forces &the next thing was to to
plant the old Stars &Stripes upon the court house & Some of the most
prominent buildings which was done in a very few minutes   Some
of the citizens hailed our flag with joy & tears while others looked
down upon it with Scorn   the union principle is rather weak in
this place but it is hourly developing itself   the rebels burned the
navy yard & Several Steam boats but they were to much hurried to
do a great deal of damage   yorktown & richmond[38] are in our
hands & the Merrimack[39] is blown up it was done by the rebel crew to
prevent her from falling into our hands   I think we will march on to
Suffolk in a few days   part of the army is already advancing in that
direction & no doubt but that is their destination   our regiment is
Still in excellent health & high Spirits   I received two letters from
wesley lately one the Sameday I received yours & one Since   he
is well &William is well also   Samuel is Sent to CinCinnatti &
perhaps home   I believe he is discharged   This is all for the
present   Please write

yours with much Love & respect
Isaac Walters[40]

[ISAAC WALTERS] TO [DAVID AND RACHEL WALTERS]

[*Front of letter remnant.*]
[*loss*] Camp in Front of Richmond
[*loss*] June the 13th /62

[*Back of letter remnant.*]
Determined in his purposes – N[*loss*]
he is most noble man I w[*loss*]
of all our estem his appear [*loss*]
proves this very plainly [*loss*][41]

ISAAC WALTERS TO DAVID AND RACHEL WALTERS

July the 8th, 1862

Dear Brother & Sister

I received your kind letter yesterday & was glad to hear from you
once more- I read your letter with much interest   I was glad to hear
of your good health & also that your father is on the mend-I think he
has had a very Severe time of it & hope he may be restored to health
again   your letter found me well but not very well contented
I am geting tired of the war-I think it is not Carried on as it Should
be   I feel very confident that this war could have been ended before
this time if properly managed   but just as long as our goverment
tries to Carry war in one hand & peace in the other just So long this
war will last & an other thing is this which I have been eye witness
to myself & which is the hardest of all-The wounded are not properly
cared for   I was cut off from my regt in a fight withe the rebels last
week & got with our Sick & wounded & could not get back to my regt
for two days So I Stayed with the Sick & wounded during this time & I
Saw as much as a hundred wounded men lying on the ground without
having their wounds dressed or cared for in any way   they werre
laying at a landing waiting transportation_ Some of them had blankets
to lay upon & others had none & I have Seen a great many thers that
had been wounded for a month & never had their wounds dressed only
as they done it themselves & Some of their arm & legs were mortifying
& them going about without Scarcely any thing to eat & had to lay on
the ground every night   Some of them had blankets & Some had
none & they had to do their own cooking & wait upon themselves as
best they could-Every time they passed any water I could See them
pooring water on their wounds to keep them from mortifying   All
this is a hard Sight to behold & this is why I Say I am tired of the
war   If it Should be my lot to get wounded in battle & treated in
this way I would choose death in preferance to living in any Such a way
but I hope this may not be my lot- I think after a Soldier has Served
faithful for a long time & then is wounded in battle he ought to be
cared for better than all this-I think goverment ought to take measures
Some way or other to provide Some quick relief for the wounded of our
once happy land   We have not got more then one fourth as many
Surgeons and waiters with the army as we ought to have-This is a good

deal the reason why the wounded are so neglected-the cant possibly get through with what they ought to do-& I cant See for my life why this vacancy is not filled- I think Some Suitable person ought to petition to our government for aid in this important respect   May God pity the wounded Soldiers   I hope this may not be my lot we have had Some very hard fighting to do lately & expect more Soon   we fought three days in Sucession.

We have fell back on the james river the enemy pursued us & we fought them all the way   our regt was in the rear & was exposed to all the enemies fire   we Suffered pretty bad   the loss in our regiment is about one hundred & fifty killed wounded & missing   Our Lieut Col is wounded & we have lost our Adjutant   we think he was taken prisoner   Our whole loss in the three days fight is estimated at 15,000 & the rebels acknowledge a loss of 40,000   it is dreadful in the extreme   I Suppose this movement in McClellan[42] will be a mystery to you all but it is no less a mystery to me-I hope it is all for the better-the officers place great confidence in him & Say it is a great move for us & will redown to great good-I hope it may be the case-you must all rest contented & See that the result will be-Although I dont think you will larn the truth of it until richmond is ours_ perhaps it may Some time before this good news will conveyed to[43]

Write Soon   I Still remain your dear & Sincere Friend   Your Ears & it may be but a very Short time-I cant tell any more than you can   We will have to rest patiently & await the result but I hope it wont be long at the furthest

I am willing to do all I can toward taking that Infernal City-We are laying here under the protection of our gun boats fortifying & preparing to give the enemy a warm reception Should they attack us   Joseph & James McCauley is well but Joseph Ferrel is not very well   he has been complaining about a week

I will close for the present
Isaac Walters[44]

DAVID W. WALTERS TO RACHEL J. WALTERS

September 01 62
[*illegible deletion*] Camp Joerusnals[45]

   I received your leter this morning and red it With much
interest   I am Well and well sadisfied   We [*illegible deletion*]
have drawd part of our uniform and ~~the~~ We Will draw the rest Soon.
and the ie our officers say We may have a furlow[46] but not ~~but~~ before
   eli is here he says he is ganneng So no more at presant

                         your friend
                         DW

                         Direct in Care of Capt B Bank
                         Banks[47]
                         I I Camp ~~Jon~~[48]

DAVID W. WALTERS TO RACHEL J. WALTERS

September the 6, 1862[49]

My dear friend,

    i take this present opportuny to rite to you let you have how we
are getting along   wee a rived here wednesday a bout 5 o clock we
had some fun a coming down here you beter believe their was a bout
30 soldiers on the cars[50] from valparraso[51] and a ten of us got on at
logonsport[52]   we change ~~once~~ cars once at cocamo[53] we have a
lected all of hour officers[54]   theire are all nice sirel men
    rachel i would not change my position with any body we have not
got hour uniform yet   we wil muster in next monday and then
we wil get them as soon as we get them we exspect to come home on
a furlow next ~~m~~ week   their is such a excitement here that know
one could get home sicke here rachel i want you to take good care of
everthing spesly of wiley and ned and fido   learn fido to bite ever
body that comes their and lern willey to dance and box and stand on
his head   it is given up that we have the best [*illegible deletion*]
company in our rigement   we wil get 23 dollars bounty[55] down
and one months wages downe whitch is 13 dollars sonomore at present
but everremain your friend   when you ~~rite~~ rite direct to camp
~~Jorunnels~~ Jorunals[56] in care of Cap banks, indianapolis

                                        Written By
                                        D.W. Walters[57]

This envelope printed with patriotic symbols of the United States carried
a letter written by David W. Walters on September 29, 1862, at Camp Joe
Reynolds, Indiana. It passed through the post office at Indianapolis and was
sent to Royal Center, where the postmaster crossed out the town's name, wrote
Rachel J. Walters's new address, and forwarded it to Star City at an additional
cost of three cents. The changed address shows one aspect of the upheaval
in Rachel J. Walters's life in the weeks following her husband's enlistment.
(*National Postal Museum, Smithsonian Institution, 0.256400.3*)

DAVID W. WALTERS TO RACHEL J. WALTERS

Camp Jo Rannels[58]
Sept 29th 1862

My dear companion,

Thru the mercys of a kind God I am permitted to drop you a few lins
to let you no that I am well & hearty   All thine and shall separates
us we can think of thins past the future is all unknown to us   there
fore we have to trust in that kind being that rules & over rules all thing
for our good   I like soaldiering fine   I have gained in flesh ever

since I am here   we have drawed our armes consisting of a saber &
revolver[59]   we will not draw our Horses for a few days & we may
not draw them this week   There is five companeys that have drawed
ther Horses & have marching orders but dont no when they will leave.
the regt is a bout full but is not fully organised   I have bin expecting
a furlow home for the last three weeks but I have given up all hopes of
geting one   you must do the best that you can   trust in God &
all will be right for he careth for him. I Still feel that warm desire for
you that I ever did & my Prayers is that we may ever be bound to gether
with that love that binds husband & wife to gether

   Wm House has bin sick or un well ever since we have him here.
he is now in the Hospital   he feels a little better than he did
yesterday   Perhaps by good treetment he will be a bout in a few
days again   The most that he complains of is a severe pain in his
brest   I am takeing the best care of him that I can & will continue
to do so as long as he needs it   this per haps is one of the main
things that we live for is to help one another in thimes of need

   We have Company drill twice in the fore noon & Batallion drill in
the after noon lasting from two till five P.M. &dress Parade at six P.M.

   There is a great many soldiers passing thru here   it has averaged
one Regt a day ever since I have bin here   There is about three
thousand five hundred in this camp   this is a regular camp of
instrucsion   all the recruits for the old Regts come here   There
is cavailry Infantry & battery all here together

   I send you $25.00   I want you to pay it to father[60]   I want you
to have father to moove you to his house & to your old home where you
will be better cared for than if you would stay a lone   I am sory it is
so that you have to fall back on ~~your~~ his care But I feel that our contry
needs my help & I am willing to do all that I can & eaven give my life
for your libertys & our beloved childs   I send my miniature &
when this you see remember me. I want you to send me yours & Willies
likeness as soon as you can   I may possibly get home but dont look
for me till you see me coming   My Eyes is still week & I want you
to send me my goggles[61] as I doubtless will need them   I allowed to
brot them ~~them~~ with me but forgot them

   I would just say that this money is for your father so that you may
understand my letter   I am a going to send my brother & my
cloathing to you soon & you will find in them a noice pair of boots
which I got for you   Clay Sellers of Fulton is here he is a recruit for
the 29th Regt   I guess that I had better bring my letter to a close

least I should weary you with my long letter   Pleas rite as soon as
you get this & let me no how you ar geting a long   I hope that the
thime is not far distant when I may again return home & enjoy your
warm in braces & pleasant smiles & sweet kises   I never new what it
was to be absent from you before but weep not for me   trust in God
& all will be rite   I would farther say that the 99th is here & that the
Roil Center[62] Boys is here   I will close by saying fare ye well for this
thime but I trust not forever   if we should not ever meet here on
this ground of sorow   let us try to live in that way that we may meet
in that world where no sorow cometh & where we will meet to part no
more

> So fare ye well
> D W Walters to
>
> Rachel J Walters
>
> Per John S Louderback[63]
>
> This ring I also send you
> D. W. W.[64]

DAVID W. WALTERS TO RACHEL J. WALTERS

Camp Joramels[65]
~~Sept~~ Oct. 1st 1862

My Dear Companion

I Just would say that I just received your letter & was veiry glad to hear from you as it has bin some thime since I head from you

I just sent you a letter monday with 25 dollars in it directed to Roialsenter[66] supposing that you was there yet so I thot that I had better drop you a few lines so that you could get it - I want you to have your fother take my things in his own hands & do with them a he sees fit & I will be satisfied

I am sory that you ar put to so much trouble with our things but it cant be helped now & I feel that I am doing my duty in helping to maintain the laws of our country & put down this wicked rebellion – My dear companion dont fret or such for me but trust in God & all will be rite.

I am well & hearty   we have fine thimes here now   we ar drilling a bout as trong & as much as we can   yesterday there was about six thousand on drill at one thime in & one boddy - to day we had about the same in nomber of soaldiers & about 30 or 40 thousand spectators

we had the biggest thime today that we have had since I have bin here   we had a regular sham battle & fired 25 rounds a piece   there was infantry cavailry & two cannon in the engagement & also a general enter view of the governor - the governor[67] is a fine looking man & I think a perfect jentleman

There is a good many of the boys wives comeing to see them & I want you ~~to come~~ & your father to come down if you can as I dont no as I will get to come at all now   Troops is passing thru now more rapped than ever   there is two standing in front of our camp now & I now just behind them - by the way that troops is passing I dont think that I will stay [illegible deletion] my thime out   there is some talk of price now whether it is gass or reality or not I cant say but one thing I do feel that I would like to go and have one round at them any way   If I aint home in one week you need not look for me at all - Come down if you can

Wm House is no better   he was taken to the Citty Hospital
Tuesday   the doctors say that he has the Tiphiod fever

I close with my best respects and well wishes to
all my friends
D. Wm Walters

To Rachel J. Walters[68]

David W. Walters to Rachel J. Walters

Camp Jo Rayanalds[69]
Oct. 7th 1862

My dear companion,

    thi s pleasant morning after my love & respects to you - I would say that I am well & hearty hopeing that these few lines may find you in the same state of health   We ar still here in camp Playing trooper dismounted.[70] we ar geting very tired of it & hope that we will draw our horses soon   Wm House is still in the hospital   I expect to be home in a few days but cant say what day as I got the promise of my capt yesterday   So you need not rite any more as I will be there at farthast against the election day[71]

    No more at preasent but still remain your affecsionate husband as ever

D. W. Walters[72]

RACHEL J. WALTERS TO DAVID W. WALTERS

Star City Pulaski Co Ind
Oct 7th /62

My Dear companion

   through the mercies of an all wise God I am permitted this morning
to address you by way of pen and paper   I have had a sore throat
but it is almost well now   Willy is not very well he is cutting teeth
which makes him very fretful but he is getting better so that he ~~go~~ can go
down and play a little but I hope when these few lines reaches you they
may find you well. I have received two letters from you lately one last
thursday evening and one monday evening the one that you directed to
Royal Center was remailed as sent on to Star city   I got the money
and the ring but I have not got the minature or clothes yet[73] O David that
ring   what beautiful present I shall keep it as a token of love and true
friendship   you stated in one of your letters that you wanted mine and
Willys minatures   I will get them as soon as I can and send them to
you   you also stated that you wanted me to send your gogles[74] but your
mother has got them and I will have to wait til I can go down there and get
them which I hope will not be many days and then I will send them to you
for I am anxious that you should have them   O David I would be so
glad to have you to come home for I want to see you so bad and it would be
so much more satisfaction to me to have you to come here than for me to
go there   you said that you wanted pap and me to come down and see
you if you could not come home   I cannot say whether we can come
or not as I have not asked pap anything about it but I expect ~~come it to~~
that he will come if he can   Mr Dickson is here   he came here last
night   he is sick with the billious fever[75] and I do not know how long he
will stay here   Mary Ann Stewarts funeral is to be preached the third
sunday by Mr. Dickson   there was no draft in this township nor in
boon township either   this is the fourth letter I have written you and I
have received four from you[76] and I would be glad to receive one every day
or two if I could for I am always glad to hear from you but I must close as
they[77] are waiting to take the letter to the office and Willy is crying for me
to take him   please write as soon as you get this   O David trust in
god and pray that he may grant you a speedy return so no more at present

from your afectionate wife
Rachel J Walters

To David W. Walters[78]

David W. Walters to Rachel J. Walters

Camp Jo Reynolds[79]
October the 27[80]

Dear wife,

It is withe pleasure that I atempt riting you those few lines   I am well and hope that when those fiew lines come to hand they may find you in the same good helth

I have riten to you once sins I have ben back[81] and have received no answer   I sent that Receipt of your Fathers and wold be glad to here whether he got it or noti   t had ben advetist and cost two dollars more which I paid with mi one money   Thare is new winter quartes which we will go in to day or tomorrow   the helth in camp is generaly good   thare was one of our boys taken to the hospitel yesterday   it was young Swete   the rest is well   thare is two of our officers under arest for neglect of thare duty   William House has come back and is ganing in helth fast

Well I believe I have writen al that will interest you   I want you should write soon   I expect we Shod Stay here all winter

As ever your Husband
D. W. Walters

R J. Walters[82]

RACHEL J. WALTERS TO DAVID W. WALTERS

Star City Pulaski Co Ind
Wednesday morning Nov 12th /62

My Dear and much loved companion

    I again take up the pen to try to answer your letter which I received
last night after dark   your letter found me well and i do hope
this may find you well. it is a mystery to me why you do not get my
letters   I have answerd every one that ~~that~~ I have received this is
the third or fourth one that I have written since you was here and you
say you have received but one   you say you have some notion of
joining the regulars[83] if I will lett you   now David as you want to
know my mind on it I will give it   David I would not have you to
join the regulars for any thing we do not any of us want you to join
them   Phebe says to tell you she says no twice, for we want you
to come home as soon as you can. it has not been quite four weeks
since I saw you and it seems to me like four months O the time seems
so long I can hardly wait   you say you want me to knit you a pair
of mittens with one finger[84]   I will knit them as soon as I can
although I hardly know how   I suppose it is the fore finger that
you want knit   I will send your handkerchief with them   I will
send you one dollar in this letter   it is all I have now   Charles
has not paid me yet we have got the corn gathered   went down on
tuesday morning and finished on friday evening there was pap and
Arthur Eddy[85] John Crane and William doud   went from here and
Springstead and his son helped one day and Bris Ring helped two days
and a half and Leonard Ring a half a day   I believe there was ten
load to our share   when we come home we tolled the hogs along
and we have got them shut up   Margaret Beckley has a fine son and
Ann Barker has a daughter Willy is well   I wish you could see how
antic he is. he can hurrah for Lincoln and play queen dido died[86] as
well as any of them O David I beg of you not to join the regulars   I
want you to come home so bad so that we can go to house keeping
again   I believe I will close for the present as I have nothing very
interesting to write you will please excuse all mistakes and my poor
writing for I am in a hurry write as often as you can and I will answer
all your letters

from your affectionate wife
Rachel J. Walters

To David W. Walters

NB Now be sure and dont join the regulars

[*Postscript is written in a different handwriting and ink color.*]
[*illegible*] Camp Carington[87]
Washington Washburn
William peman this is not but hard hard
Walters[88]

Isaac Walters to Rachel J. Walters

Dec. the. 1st /62
Camp Near Falmouth.V.A.

Dear & Much respected Sister

After this long delay to Seat myself once more to drop a few lines to you in answer to your kind letter which I received Some time ago but have not had an opportunity of writing until the present time So I hope you will not think hard of me for not writing Sooner. Your letter found me well although I have been Sick Since that time but am well now, I was very Sorry to hear of your ill health & also that david had gone to the war   I think he will rue it before long   I think he ought to Stayed at home by all means. if I Should have been placed in his circumstances I would have Stayed at home   I think it would have been more credit to him to have taken care of his family than to have gone to the army - but every one to their own notion as the old maid Said when She kissed the cow   We have been laying Still now for about one week we are on one Side of the Aque Creek[89] & the rebels on the other Side. we are in gun Shot of each other but all remains quiet.

How long we will lay Still I am unable to Say but I dont care if it all winter for I have been in just as many battles as I care about being in very Soon   for my part I can get along very well without trying it again   I hope this trouble will be compromised & Settled before long   the Sooner the better for I dont believe it ever will be Settled by the force of arms & I think it might as well be compromised first as last. it is all a money making Scheme any way & it had better be Stopped & the Sooner the better. We have had very pleasant weather here this fall but it is raining to day & has the appearance of a hard Storm but it is So late we need not expect any thing else now. Elis health is very poor   he has the Rheumatism   he is in the hospital with the regiment   I Saw him this morning   I think he is improving Slowly   The health generally in the army is good   Gen. Burnsides[90] has command of the army at the present time. I hope the war will be Settled this winter So the poor Soldiers can return to their homes next Spring. I will live in hope of the Same any how   We Still have our Shelter tents & it is very cold being in these tents this weather   I hope we will get into winter quarters[91] before long

When you write I want you to tell me where David is So I can write to him   Charles Wooley told me they had their horses Sent to Washington City & they were going to Stay at Indianapolis this winter but this dont read to me   it Seems Strange to me why they would do any Such thing as that it wouldnt give them any chance to drill or any thing else   for my part I cant believe the Story for it dont look reasonable to me   I would as Soon believe Something else Please write Soon & dont do as I done   Give all the news

I will close for the present hoping to meet you before long in Friendship True

Excuse my Short Letter

Yours until Death
Isaac Walters

To. R.J. Walters[92]

DAVID W. WALTERS TO RACHEL J. WALTERS

Camp Near Risingsun[93]
Dec. 25th 1862

Dear Wife,

This is Christmas & drole one it is to what I am used to   it is
warm & raining   the boys are enjoying them selves very well laying
round in their respective tents some riting some telling fish storieys
[*illegible deletion*] & some doing one thing & some another
        the health of the company is good only three being
sick   Collonel Williams of riseing sun has volunteered to come to
our camp onse a day to attend to the sick   we are well treated by the
[*illegible deletion*] citizens   they bring in something every day for
the sick   this morning we had a large trey of sausage sent to us for a
Christmas gift   they have promised us a new years dinner   we
face here a goodeal better than we did at Camp Carington   our
vituals is better & more of them we ar camped two miles west of Rising
sun 14 miles from Laurenceberg & 96 miles below Cincinattia   I
stood the trip well   the first night I stayed in camp carington ~~ton~~
then we came to Laurenceberg & from there I walked a good part of the
way to our camp
        this is a ritch county &vairy healthy but it is broken &
hilly   there seems to be but little yet wh a bout the people
here   the most of them is well off & live in old log houses   some
have brick bildings but loosely finished
        We ar in Ohio county   Riseing sun is the county town Rising
sun is a very moise place there is about 23 hundred inhabitance and well
supplied with churches one Baptist one Christian two Presbyterian
one Methodist & one universalist   there is a good seminary here
with about two hundred scholars   the boats still run regular & will
continue to do so as long as the river is open   there is no regular
soaldiers here except our company[94]   there is about 15 hundred
home guard & legions in this county   they are fully organised &
reddy to turn out at any call   we expect to have some thing to do
before long as the secesh is geting quite saucey   they ar begining to
act about as they did last summer before Morgan[95] come in   they
say that they ar looking for a heavy secesh forse thrown in before long

pleas rite as often as you can   take good care of your self &
child   direct your letters to ~~Riseing Sun~~ Camp near Riseingsun
Company I 5th Cavailry Ind. Vol.   so I will close

I remain yours as ever
David Walters[96]

NOTES

1. McPherson, *Battle Cry of Freedom*, 179, 230–233.

2. US National Homes for Disabled Volunteer Soldiers, 1866–1938, Isaac Walters, Pvt., Co. F, 20 Ind. Inf.; Civil War, RG 15; NA-Washington.

3. Billings, *Hardtack and Coffee*, 43–44; Gilbreath and Lane, *Dignity of Duty*, 8–11.

4. Inconsistent details about John Wesley Walters appear in his military service records. He was described as having dark hair, but some records listed a dark complexion while others listed fair; his eyes were either gray or blue; height either five feet, ten inches or five feet, six inches; and his occupation was either farmer or farrier. (Compiled military service record, John Wesley Walters, Pvt., Co. I, 46 Ind. Inf.; Civil War, RG 94; NA-Washington.)

5. Eli Walters had married in 1858 and was a farmer. At almost thirty-two years old, he was five feet, ten inches in height and had a dark complexion, dark hair, and blue eyes. (Compiled military service record, Eli Walters, Pvt., Co. F, 20 Ind. Inf.; Civil War, RG 94; NA-Washington.)

6. Compiled military service record, David W. Walters, Pvt., Co. I, 5 Ind. Cav.; Civil War, RG 94; NA-Washington.

7. The physical descriptions for the men of the Walters family come from their military service records. Of Rachel's appearance little is recorded, except that David commented on her photograph as "very hansome" in his April 26, 1864, letter (1991.0291.39), and in her letter of February 10, 1864 (1991.0291.54), she reported her weight as "one hundred and thirty lbs."

8. Billings, *Hardtack and Coffee*, 97.

9. Giesberg, *Army at Home*, 20.

10. Billings, *Hardtack and Coffee*, 164–216.

11. Fort Hatteras, located on the Outer Banks of North Carolina, was constructed by the Confederate military to protect the area for shipping but was taken by Union troops in August 1861 and held for the rest of the war. The Twen-

tieth Indiana was ordered there as part of the buildup of Union forces in the area.

12. Willard Oscar Walters was born on September 15, 1861, to David and Rachel Walters. His nickname appears as both Willy and Willie throughout the correspondence collection.

13. In the nineteenth century, *neuralgia* described ailments such as nerve pain, headaches, and discomfort.

14. According to Ina Dixon's "Modern Medicine's Civil War Legacy," sickness killed almost two-thirds of all Union and Confederate soldiers who died during the war. Poor rations, inadequate sanitation, and close camp environments allowed diseases such as typhoid fever and tuberculosis to spread rapidly throughout the ranks. Those wounded during battles also faced numerous medical challenges. Military weaponry used in the war led to the need for amputations, introducing the risk of infection. The number of wounded overwhelmed the available surgeons and physicians. Early in the conflict, soldiers were often evacuated to the nearest city to receive treatment, causing a great delay for those needing aid. As the war continued, field hospitals provided treatment closer to the battlefield. In some cases, soldiers on furlough went home to recover and alleviate burdens on the army's medical services.

15. Colonel William L. Brown, from Logansport, Indiana, was the commander of the Twentieth Indiana. He received his commission as colonel on July 23, 1861, and commanded the regiment until his death during the Battle of Second Bull Run (Manassas) on August 29, 1862.

16. A matching envelope has not been identified for this letter (1992.0291.65).

17. Camp Hamilton was located near Fortress Monroe in Hampton, Virginia.

18. During the Civil War, *pickets* were soldiers who served as guards for their regiment's camps. Pickets tended to be stationed in a large circle around a camp, enabling them to detect approaching threats and provide advance notice.

19. Felix K. Zollicoffer was a Confederate brigadier general who was mortally wounded at the Battle of Mill Springs in Kentucky on January 19, 1862.

20. John Wesley Walters, the younger brother of Isaac and David Walters, was also referred to as Wesley or Wes in the letters and signed his correspondence "J. W."

21. Martha Walters, a sister of Isaac and David Walters.

22. Hannah (McCarty) Walters.

23. The envelope (0.256400.1) for this letter (1991.0291.66) was postmarked "OLD PO[INT CO]MFORT / VA / JAN / 27" over a three-cent George Washington stamp. It was addressed "Mrs. Rachel. J. Walters / Royal. Center / Cass Co / Indiana." It was embossed on the front left with a portrait of "GEN.L Mc-CLELLAN" holding a US flag, and the edges of the envelope's flaps are colored

red and blue. The letter was written on blue-lined stationery embossed with a paper manufacturer's mark of a horse set above a crown.

24. *Miniature* is a period term for a photograph. Before the Civil War, great advancements in materials and techniques began to make photographs easier to produce and more affordable. Sitting for photographic portraits and exchanging them proliferated as military personnel and civilians sought remembrances of loved ones. One popular method of photography involved the creation of a negative and printing of the image on card stock. Multiple inexpensive copies of this type, known as a carte de viste, could be made, and portraits of well-known politicians and generals were sold to the public. Two other common photographic methods included the ambrotype and tintype (also known as ferrotype). An ambrotype consisted of an image captured on a piece of glass, the reverse being covered in black lacquer to allow the image to be clearly seen. A tintype consisted of an image captured on a thin piece of chemical-coated iron. Tintypes were durable, relatively inexpensive, and could be created in the field, resulting in thousands of soldiers having their picture taken (Zeller, *The Blue and the Gray in Black and White*, 20–21).

25. No date or location is given on the letter, but the envelope paired with this letter was postmarked March 4. It is likely the message dates from late February or early March 1862, based on Isaac Walters's description of moving to Newport News, Virginia. The envelope (1991.0291.68) for this letter (1991.0291.67) was postmarked "OLD POINT COMFORT / VA / MAR / 4" over a three-cent George Washington stamp. It was addressed "Mrs. Rachel. J. Walters / Royal. Center / Cass. Co. Ind." The letter was written on patriotic stationery with a blue-and-red-printed illustration of an American flag and smoking cannon captioned, "BABY WAKER 1776. 1861."

26. Camp Butler, Newport News, Virginia. While in Newport News on March 8, 1862, the Twentieth Indiana witnessed naval history—the first-ever engagement between ironclad warships. After attacking Union ships off the coast of Hampton Roads, Virginia, on March 8, the Confederate ironclad CSS *Virginia* (built on the hull of a US ship formerly known as the USS *Merrimack* that was captured by Confederates when the US Navy abandoned Norfolk, Virginia, at the outbreak of the war) engaged the USS *Monitor*, the Union navy's ironclad, in battle on March 9, 1862. After a four-hour engagement, both ships retreated in a draw, having struck each other twenty times with cannonballs without causing significant damage (McPherson, *War on the Waters*, 97–105).

27. Major General John E. Wool, the commander of the Department of Virginia in the US Army, was one of the oldest generals to serve during the war.

28. Fortress Monroe, located off the coast of Virginia, was held by the Union army for the duration of the war. It was often used as a staging ground for Union attacks towards Richmond, Virginia.

29. Joseph K. F. Mansfield, a brigadier general at the time of this letter, was the overall commander of the area where Isaac Walters was stationed.

30. There are no letters in the collection by Eli Walters, an older brother of Isaac and David Walters. Although Isaac Walters wrote of "Cousin Jacob," the roster in Indiana and William Terrell's *Report of the Adjutant General* for Company F, Twentieth Indiana only includes a third man with the surname Walters whose first name was Joseph and only one man by the name Jacob but whose surname was Shell (pages 421–422). Isaac did not mention "Cousin Jacob" again but later sent news about a Joseph Walters in his June 8, 1864, letter (1991.0291.88).

31. *Consumption* is a period term for the bacterial infectious disease known as tuberculosis.

32. The envelope (1991.0291.70) for this letter (1991.0291.69) was postmarked "OLD POINT COMFORT / VA / MAR / 26" over a three-cent George Washington stamp placed in the lower left corner. It was addressed "Rachel. J. Walters / Royal. Center / Cass. Co / Ind." The letter was written on blue-lined stationery embossed with a paper manufacturer's mark.

33. Phebe A. Ward, younger sister of Rachel J. (Ward) Walters.

34. Osceola, Arkansas.

35. John Wesley described the naval Battle at Fort Pillow, Tennessee, also known as the Engagement at Plum Point Bend, on May 10, 1862. Fort Pillow is better known as the site of a massacre that occurred later in the war, when on April 12, 1864, Confederate cavalry commanded by Confederate general Nathan Bedford Forrest surrounded and attacked the Union garrison of about six hundred men, about 65 percent of whom were former enslaved men serving in the US Colored Troops. Many of these soldiers were massacred after surrendering, and news of the slaughter spread throughout the nation. According to *Fort Pillow* by John Cimprich, the US government later adjusted policies related to African American soldiers, including equity of pay, as a reaction to public sentiment about the event (pages 70–85, 104).

36. *Cecesh*, or *sesech*, was a period term derived from the word *secessionist*, for a person who supported the secession of the states that became the Confederacy.

37. The letter (1991.0291.71) was written on stationery embossed with a bird on a branch mark of a paper manufacturer. A matching envelope has not been identified.

38. Yorktown, Virginia, was captured. Contrary to Isaac Walters's account in this letter, however, the Union did not take the city of Richmond during the Peninsula Campaign of 1862.

39. Isaac Walters described the destruction of the Confederate ironclad CSS *Virginia* using its earlier designation, the USS *Merrimack*, which Confederate

forces had rechristened the CSS *Virginia* after salvaging and building on the burned hull left by retreating Union troops when they abandoned Norfolk, Virginia, in April 1861. James McPherson cited in *War on the Water* (page 109) that on May 11, 1862, Confederate troops blew up the CSS *Virginia* to prevent the ship's capture as Union troops took Norfolk during the Peninsula Campaign.

40. The envelope (1991.0291.73) for this letter (1991.0291.72) was postmarked "[N]ORFORK / VA / MAY / 19" over a three-cent George Washington stamp placed upside down on the lower left corner. It was addressed "David W Walters / Royal Center / Cass Co / Ind." The pencil notation "May 18, 1863, from Isaac" was added, likely by a family member, after the letter was received and before it was donated to the museum. The letter was written on blue-lined stationery embossed with an oval-shaped mark of a paper manufacturer.

41. This small remnant of a letter (1991.0291.177.2) on blue-lined paper was torn on the left and bottom with only a couple lines of text remaining on both sides. It has handwriting like that of Isaac Walters, and records of his regiment place him in Virginia on the date of the letter. Given that Isaac wrote letters to his brother David and sister-in-law Rachel in the summer of 1862, this remnant was likely part of a letter sent to one or both. The envelope (1991.0291.177.1) in the collection that is associated with the remnant letter is also torn, on the right side only. However, it has a later date of use: a postmaster wrote "Star City Sept 30" and cancelled the three-cent George Washington stamp using black ink. The sender used blue ink to write "In haste" and addressed it "Mr David W. Walters / 5th cavalry regiment / of Indiana voluntee[*loss*] / in care of capt / Banks. Camp / Journals, Indianapo[*loss*]." The handwriting is like that of Rachel Walters, who frequently used blue ink. It cannot be determined if Rachel enclosed the June 13, 1862, letter in the envelope for her husband and dated it September 30 or whether a family member stored the two items together before donating the collection to the museum.

42. Major General George B. McClellan rose to prominence during the buildup of Union forces at the start of the war and led the Union to victory at the Battle of Philippi, June 3, 1861. He commanded the Union army in the Peninsula Campaign at the time of this letter. The July 8, 1862, letter by Isaac Walters bookends his participation in one of the war's first major campaigns, which was named for the land between the York and James Rivers over which the Union army was to advance northwest to capture the capital of the Confederacy—Richmond, Virginia. The campaign commenced in April 1862 with the siege of the city of Yorktown, Virginia. Confederate forces retreated during the evening of May 3, 1862, and Isaac Walters mentioned the capture of Yorktown in his May 18, 1862, letter. Confederate commander Joseph E. Johnston continued his retreat toward Richmond, maneuvering and skirmishing with the Union troops to slow their advance so defenses could be prepared around the capital.

On May 31, Johnston attacked McClellan's forces during the Battle of Seven Pines after learning that the Union army was split by the Chickahominy River. The battle halted McClellan's advance, but Johnston was wounded during the offensive action. Confederate general Robert E. Lee was placed in command and set to work on fortifications and maneuvering the forces into positions to defend against the Union army. After fierce fighting on June 25 and June 26, McClellan decided to withdraw back down the Virginia peninsula. Lee pursued McClellan in a series of bloody battles known as the Seven Days, until early July, when the Union army reached Harrison's Landing, where it was protected by the Union navy. The Union army was eventually withdrawn from the area in August. Both armies suffered heavy casualties—the Union had over fifteen thousand casualties and the Confederate forces almost twenty thousand. Although more costly in manpower for the Confederacy, Richmond was defended and the Union army forced to retreat (Sears, *To the Gates of Richmond*, 1–2, 5, 68–72, 111–177, 344–345).

43. Isaac Walters was referring to the Union forces' retreat from the outskirts of Richmond, Virginia, after engaging in the Seven Days Battles with Confederate forces, June 25 to July 1, 1862.

44. Based on the date and Isaac Walters's description in this letter, he likely wrote this near Harrison's Landing, Virginia. The letter (1991.0291.75) was dispatched through Washington, DC, where the envelope (1991.0291.76) was postmarked "WA[SHING]TON / [D.C.] / JU[L *illegible*]" to the left of a cancelled three-cent George Washington stamp. "U.S. Sanitary Commission" was printed in the upper left corner, and the envelope was addressed "Mrs. Rachel. J. Walters / Star City / Pulaski Co. / Ind." The letter was written on two sheets of paper.

45. Camp Joe Reynolds, Indianapolis, Indiana.

46. During the Civil War, a soldier could request a furlough, but the military primarily granted this type of temporary leave of absence to allow personnel to return home for a short period due to illness, as recognition for extraordinary action, as an incentive with a new enlistment, or as an inducement for reenlistment. Some states encouraged military units to allow furloughs so soldiers could return home to vote in elections. Indiana's Governor Morton promoted soldiers' furloughs during the 1864 presidential election.

47. Ephraim N. Banks, from Rochester, Indiana, was captain of Company I, Fifth Indiana Cavalry at the time of this letter. It was common for mail to be addressed to a unit's commander, who typically oversaw the handling of mail because soldiers and officers did not have permanent addresses.

48. The envelope (1991.0291.2) for this letter (1991.0291.1) was postmarked "IN[DIANAPOLIS] / IND / S[EP] / [*illegible*]" over a three-cent George Washington stamp. A "Due 3" handstamp indicates that additional postage was

required because this mail weighed over half an ounce but less than one ounce. It is addressed "Royalcenter ind / R. J. Walters." The pencil notation "1862" was added, likely by a family member, after the letter was received and before it was donated to the museum. The letter was written in pencil on blue-lined paper.

49. The Fifth Indiana Cavalry was mustered into service on this date at Camp Joe Reynolds.

50. *Cars* refers to rail cars. Railway lines played a vital role during the Civil War by carrying soldiers, supplies, and equipment. The swift movement of troops and materiel proved essential to the outcome of numerous campaigns.

51. Valparaiso, Indiana.

52. Logansport, Indiana.

53. Kokomo, Indiana.

54. Practices for selecting officers varied among the earliest volunteer regiments to be formed. Some volunteers believed they should have the right to vote for their officers as they did for political seats, and these units elected officers. In other cases, governors granted officer commissions as favors. Regardless of how they were chosen, the lack of military training and presumptive attitudes that the necessary skills could be learned quickly led to disasters in the first months of the war. After these initial setbacks, the US Congress formed review boards for officers, and some were discharged or resigned when it was found that they lacked the skills to command. By 1863, the Union army was generally not electing officers anymore, though some were still commissioned by governors (McPherson, *Battle Cry of Freedom*, 326–327).

55. In order to meet the recruiting quotas set by the US government, many states offered bounties in the form of cash bonuses to encourage enlistment. The military records of David Walters note that he was to receive a bounty and premium in the amount of twenty-seven dollars. (Compiled military service record, David W. Walters, Pvt., Co. I, 5 Ind. Cav.; Civil War, RG 94; NA-Washington.)

56. Camp Joe Reynolds, Indiana.

57. The envelope (1991.0291.4) for this letter (1991.0291.3) was postmarked "[IND]IANAPOLIS / [IND] / SEP / 8 / 1[862]" in the upper right corner. The cancelled three-cent George Washington stamp was placed on its side on the upper left corner. It was addressed between wavy, hand-drawn lines: "Royalcenter / R. J. Walters / Ind." Two notations, "first letter" and "from David," were added, likely by a family member, after the letter was received and before it was donated to the museum. The letter was written in pencil on blue-lined stationery embossed with a paper manufacturer's mark.

58. Camp Joe Reynolds, Indiana.

59. The saber and revolver were standard equipment for Union cavalrymen, some of whom were also armed with carbines and repeating rifles.

60. Samuel Ward Jr., father of Rachel J. (Ward) Walters.

61. *Goggles* is a period term for eyewear protection against sunlight and other elements.

62. Royal Center, Indiana.

63. John S. Louderback was a member of David Walters's company. The line "per John S Louderback" may signify that he penned the letter for David or indicate that he was to bring Rachel Walters some of the items that her husband, David, described. It was not uncommon for soldiers returning home on furlough to help their comrades by delivering messages and goods, particularly material, like the clothing mentioned here, that would have exceeded the mail's weight limits.

64. The letter's handwriting shows characteristics in common with that of John S. Louderback's letters in the collection and differs from the two short letters sent by David Walters earlier in September 1862 (1991.0291.1 and 1991.0291.3). The envelope (0.256400.3) for this letter (1991.0291.5), which was written on two sheets of blue-lined stationery embossed with a paper manufacturer's mark, has a red-and-blue-printed seal of the United States that dominates the left half of the envelope and is surrounded by abbreviations for thirty-four states. It is addressed "Rachel J Walters / ~~Roilcenter PO / Cass Co / Ind~~ / Star City / Ind." The three-cent George Washington stamp, which was placed on its side in the lower left corner and is postmarked "INDIANAPOLIS / IND / [Sep] / 30 / 186[2]," was sufficient postage for delivery to the Royal Center post office, but, as evident from the "forwarded" notation along the lower edge and the change in the address, the mail was sent on to Star City. This required an additional three cents, and the stamp for the second journey is in the lower right corner with a postmark, "ROYAL CENTER / IND / OCT / 2."

65. Camp Joe Reynolds, Indiana.

66. Royal Center, Indiana.

67. Oliver P. Morton, a Republican and close ally of Abraham Lincoln, was governor of Indiana during the Civil War.

68. The handwriting in this letter has characteristics in common with that of John S. Louderback's letters in the collection. The envelope (0.256400.5) for this letter (1991.0291.6), which was written on blue-lined stationery embossed with an eagle, has a three-cent George Washington stamp in the lower left corner that is postmarked "INDI[ANAPOLIS] / IND / OCT / 2 / 1862." It was addressed "Rachel J Walters / Star City PO / Ind." A red-and-blue-printed seal of the United States dominates the left half of the envelope and is surrounded by abbreviations for thirty-four states.

69. Camp Joe Reynolds, Indiana.

70. A cavalry unit without horses was called dismounted. In some cases, a cavalry unit received orders to fight without horses, wherein three out of every

four members would fight like infantry soldiers, and the fourth man would hold the horses. In other cases, such as this one, units were waiting to be issued horses, or reissued new horses, if in need of mounts.

71. The state election was scheduled for October 14, 1862.

72. The handwriting in this letter has characteristics in common with that of John S. Louderback's letters in the collection. The envelope (0.256400.4) for this letter (1991.0291.7), which was written on blue-lined paper, has a three-cent George Washington stamp placed on its side in the lower left corner. It was postmarked "INDIANA[POLIS] / IND / OCT / 7 / 1862" and was addressed "Rachel. J. Walters / Starcitty / Ind." A red-and-blue-printed seal of the United States dominates the left half of the envelope and is surrounded by abbreviations for thirty-four states.

73. David Walters's letter of September 29, 1862 (1991.0291.5), described his intentions to send twenty-five dollars, a ring, a miniature, and clothing to his wife, Rachel. His postscript, "per John S Louderback," may have indicated that his comrade would deliver some of the items that David did not enclose with the letter. Rachel listed the items she did not receive with the letter.

74. Rachel Walters was answering her husband, David's, request for photographs and goggles in his September 29 letter.

75. *Bilious fever* was a period term for illnesses causing elevated temperatures and gastrointestinal symptoms.

76. No earlier letters written by Rachel Walters in 1862 exist in the collection. There are four letters in the collection by David Walters that predate this and a fifth letter written by him on the same date.

77. *They* likely refers to a family member who was going to the post office. Letter writers commonly remarked on the timing of trips to the post office and emphasized their alacrity in writing and sending correspondence.

78. The letter (1991.0291.42) was written in blue ink on blue-lined paper. A matching envelope has not been identified.

79. Camp Joe Reynolds, Indiana.

80. No year is written on this letter, but it is likely 1862 because David Walters was at Camp Joe Reynolds that autumn.

81. In his letter of October 7 (1991.0291.7), David Walters had anticipated returning home by the state election day, October 14, 1862.

82. The envelope (1991.0291.9) for this letter (1991.0291.8), which was written on stationery with a scene from the Battle of Cedar Mountain printed in black with the caption "Brilliant Engagement of General Banks' Division with Rebel forces under Stonewall Jackson, August 9th, 1862," had a three-cent George Washington stamp placed on its side in the upper right corner and is postmarked "I[NDIANAPOLIS] / IND / O[CT] / 27 / 1862." It was addressed "Miss R J Walters / Star city / Indiana." The pencil notation "Pulaski County"

was added, likely by a family member, after the letter was received and before it was donated to the museum. An illustration on the envelope's left side printed in blue and red depicts an officer on horseback leading troops carrying American flags and includes a poem:

> We are coming, Father Abraham,
> Six hundred thousand more,
> From Mississippi's winding stream,
> And from New England's shore.
> We leave our ploughs and workshops,
> Our wives and children dear,
> With hearts too full for utterance,
> With but a silent tear.
> We will not look behind us,
> But steadfastly before.
> We are coming, father Abraham,
> Six hundred thousand more!

83. This refers to the regular army, which was the professional army of the United States, as opposed to the volunteer regiments raised by individual states during the war.

84. Known as trigger-finger mittens, they were not issued to soldiers as part of their uniforms and equipment, but many chose to purchase or ask their family for them. They were like traditional mittens except the index finger had its own sheath like that of the thumb. This allowed soldiers to wear mittens in cold weather yet still fire their rifles with their index finger.

85. *Pap and Arthur Eddy* refers to Rachel J. (Ward) Walters's father, Samuel, and younger brothers, Arthur M. and William Edwin Ward.

86. Queen Dido Died was a children's game played by adding and repeating phrases and motions.

87. Camp Carrington, Indianapolis, Indiana, was established in 1862.

88. The letter (1991.0291.43) was written on blue-lined paper, and the handwriting in blue ink was by Rachel Walters. The four lines written in brown ink at the end of the letter are similar to David Walters's penmanship. A matching envelope has not been identified.

89. Aquia Creek.

90. Ambrose E. Burnside started the war as a colonel of the First Rhode Island Infantry. He participated in the campaign against Confederate forces in coastal North Carolina and eventually rose to the rank of major general. At the time of this letter, Major General Burnside was in command of the Union Army of the Potomac, having taken over after President Abraham Lincoln dismissed

Major General George B. McClellan from command following the Battle of An-
tietam, September 16–18, 1862.

91. During the winter, soldiers would often set up semipermanent log huts
with fireplaces to help keep warm. When on a campaign, soldiers carried tents
for shelter and sometimes opted to sleep without them (Billings, *Hardtack and
Coffee*, 43–60).

92. The envelope (1991.0291.78) for this letter (1991.0291.77) was postmarked
"WASHINGTO[N CI]TY / DEC / 8" over a three-cent George Washington
stamp. It was addressed "Mrs. Rachel. J. Walters / Star City / Pulaski. Co.
Ind." The pencil notation "from Isaac / Dec 1 – 62" was added, likely by a family
member, after the letter was received and before it was donated to the museum.
The letter was written on blue-lined stationery embossed with a paper manufacturer's mark.

93. The Fifth Indiana Cavalry arrived at Camp Williams, near Rising Sun,
Indiana, on December 25, 1862.

94. David Walters was not describing the permanent, regular army of the
United States, but instead he made the distinction that his volunteer regiment
was a military unit as opposed to a militia or home guard unit.

95. Brigadier General John Hunt Morgan commanded Confederate cavalry
known for guerrilla attacks on Union supply lines and depots throughout Tennessee and Kentucky in 1862. The citizens of Indiana were concerned with the
possibility of attacks into the state. Governor Oliver Morton organized the state
militia, known as the Indiana Legion, to try to defend the border from raids.

96. The handwriting in this letter has characteristics in common with that
of John S. Louderback's letters in the collection. The envelope (1991.0291.11) for
this letter (1991.0291.10) was postmarked "[RISI]NG SUN / [In]d. / DEC," and
pencil notations "25" and "1862" were added, likely by a family member, after
the letter was received and before it was donated to the museum. A three-cent
George Washington stamp in the upper left corner has a cancellation mark, and
the envelope is addressed "Mrs Davit Walters / Roilcenter Post / Cassco / Ind."
The letter was written in pencil on laid paper with blue lines.

THREE

—◊◊◊—

1863

Health is a great blessing any where but it is a greater one in the army than any place else for it is a very poor place for a Sick man any person not having a good Constitution had better stay out of the army.

—Isaac Walters to his sister-in-law Rachel J. Walters, September 26, 1863

AT THE CLOSE OF 1862, Eli Walters returned home with a medical discharge for rheumatism. He had served for about four months alongside his younger brother Isaac. For Isaac Walters, the turn of the year saw him spending a second winter in the field. The Twentieth Indiana recuperated in Virginia following the Battle of Fredericksburg, December 11–15, 1862. Three weeks after the Union forces retreated, Isaac mentioned the battle to his sister-in-law Rachel Walters but did not send details.

Taking a different approach to handling difficult news, Rachel relied on details when writing to her husband, David, in May 1863. David's mother, Hannah (McCarty) Walters, had died suddenly, and Rachel carefully recounted for David the specifics provided to her in letters sent by a friend and her sister-in-law, Martha Walters. She described Hannah's last moments, the subsequent inquest, and burial. Rachel had missed the funeral because she was not informed in time to attend. Returning home for the memorial was not an option for her husband, who was serving in Kentucky at the time. Correspondence was the only way Rachel and David could share the loss while separated by distance and the war.

The spring also saw the death of Isaac Dunkin, who had been married to Rachel Walters's sister Phebe for only two months. Again, Rachel kept the family informed. John Wesley Walters replied with his sympathies in his June 10, 1863, letter, and despite being in the same regiment, Isaac Walters could not recall his

BATTLE OF CHAMPION HILLS, MAY 16, 1863.—THE POSITION OF GENERAL PEMBERTON CARRIED BY GENERALS HOVEY, LOGAN AND CROCKER, OF GENERAL GRANT'S ARMY.

This illustration of the Battle of Champion Hill, May 16, 1863, appeared in *The Civil War in the United States* in 1884. A personal account of the battle served as the subject of John Wesley Walters's letter to his sister-in-law Rachel on June 10, 1863, in which he described the Forty-Sixth Indiana's actions and the wounds he sustained. *(Courtesy of Thomas J. Paone)*

acquaintance with Dunkin, but his comrade remembered him in the regiment, as Isaac recounted in his September 26, 1863, letter.

Sometimes the tumultuous course of events affected the reliability of information imparted by trusted friends and family. The rumor—passed from a community member to Rachel then to David in her June 8, 1863, letter—of John Wesley's death in the spring of 1863 came prematurely. In truth, John Wesley had survived the Battle of Champion Hill on May 16, 1863, which was a key engagement in the Vicksburg Campaign.[1] John Wesley sustained injuries to his hand and hip. On June 10, he sent a blow-by-blow account of the combat to his sister-in-law while he recuperated at a hospital in Memphis, Tennessee. While John Wesley recovered, his regiment fought in the siege of Vicksburg until July 4, 1863, when the Confederate forces finally surrendered after troops and civilians had endured months of bombardment and starvation. The fall of Vicksburg gave Union forces complete access to the Mississippi River and movement of warships, troops, and supplies, effectively splitting the Confederacy in two, which greatly weakened its ability to fight the war.[2]

"Morgan's Raid into Indiana—The Confederate Guerillas Destroying and Pillaging the Depot and Stores at Salem, Indiana, July 10" was published in *Frank Leslie's Illustrated Newspaper*, August 8, 1863. Civilians in Indiana, Kentucky, and Ohio felt terrorized by Confederate brigadier general John Hunt Morgan's raids during the summer of 1863. The pursuit of the insurgents featured in many of David W. Walters's letters, including his July 22 account of one of the final fights against Morgan's troops. *(General Photograph Collection, Rare Books and Manuscripts, Indiana State Library)*

Farther east, David encountered almost constant action and movement in the summer of 1863 as his regiment tracked Confederate brigadier general John Hunt Morgan, whose troops were raiding and terrorizing civilians of several states. In July 1863, the noted cavalry commander captured two steamboats and crossed the Ohio River into Indiana with approximately 2,500 troops after riding through Kentucky. Morgan's troops swept across southern Indiana and the southern border of Ohio, engaging with state militia soldiers, pillaging supplies, and causing fear and anxiety in the populace. The raids came to an end near the eastern Pennsylvania border when Union soldiers blocked the escape of the raiders during the Battles of Buffington Island, July 19, 1863, and Salineville, July 26, 1863, capturing Morgan and most of the Confederate forces that remained after the campaign.[3]

David Walters and the Fifth Indiana Cavalry stayed in the volatile area of Kentucky, which was increasingly susceptible to insurgent attacks as political sympathies continued to shift. Kentucky was one of several border states, which, along with Missouri and Maryland, were critical to both the Union and

This love token, inscribed "Our hearts" and made of entwined white and green papers, may have been enclosed in David W. Walters's July 22, 1863, letter to his wife, Rachel. It is unknown who created the piece and for whom it was intended. *(National Postal Museum, Smithsonian Institution, 1991.0291.19)*

Confederacy. (Delaware was also technically a border state, but with less than 2 percent of its population enslaved, the state had a strong Union sentiment.) Although Kentucky did not secede, state officials declared Kentucky neutral and refused President Abraham Lincoln's call for soldiers to the Union army. The white, male Kentuckians who eventually enlisted, like those from Missouri and Maryland, volunteered for both armies, with about two-fifths of the volunteers joining the Confederate forces.[4] At first, both Union and Confederate militaries refrained from sending troops into the state, but this changed after the unofficial truce between the armies ended on September 3, 1861, when Confederate troops under the command of Leonidas Polk entered Kentucky. Union troops under the command of Ulysses Grant countered this movement. As a result of the Confederate forces' initial move, public sentiment in Kentucky rose in favor of the Union cause.[5]

Federal troops sought to maintain political and public control of Kentucky by declaring martial law and firmly establishing a military presence in the state. Concerned about the upcoming state election in August, Major General Ambrose Burnside of the Army of the Ohio declared martial law on July 31, 1863, in response to the Confederate incursion and to protect voters from potential intimidation and interference.[6] The regimental commander of the Fifth Indiana Cavalry similarly declared martial law over the citizens of Bardstown and Nelson counties as of August 1, 1863. On that same day, David Walters sent home a print of his regiment's special order and shared the news of the instability he and his regiment were sent to quell.

Meanwhile, David Walters's brother Isaac faced grueling battles in the Eastern Theater. The Twentieth Indiana participated in the Chancellorsville and Gettysburg Campaigns.[7] The regiment was heavily engaged on the second day of the Battle of Gettysburg, July 1–3, 1863, and suffered severe casualties, especially among its officers.[8] The lack of correspondence from Isaac during this period may have resulted from his regiment's near-constant campaigning.

By the time Isaac Walters penned his September 26 letter, he was garrisoned at Fort Schulyer in the Bronx, New York. Following the Union's victory at Gettysburg and the pursuit of Confederate forces back to Virginia, the Twentieth Indiana was detached from the army and assigned duties in New York City in August. It was one of several regiments tasked to keep the peace after riots erupted in protest of the first draft, which took place in July. The government, needing to fill the ranks with able-bodied men as the war dragged on and casualties mounted, had passed the Enrollment Act in March 1863.[9] The new conscription law inflamed simmering resentment of the war among both lower-income workers who could not afford to pay the $300 commutation fee or find a substitute enrollee and those who opposed the war shifting from one focused on keeping the Union intact to one that also included a fight for the emancipation of enslaved people.

In New York City, draft officers began drawing names on July 11, 1863. Tensions were high, especially among the Irish, who largely held low-skilled jobs and feared potential competition from freed slaves and who could not afford draftee substitutes or commutation. On July 13, violent protests broke out throughout the city. Rioters set draft offices on fire, attacked newspaper printing offices and churches, and burned the Colored Orphan Asylum to the ground. African

Americans lost their homes and lives in the violence and were the vast majority of the over one hundred reported deaths as mobs targeted people of color. Police officers and militia troops could do little to stop the mob. Military regiments that had just participated in the Battle of Gettysburg were rushed to New York to help. By July 17, the violence was mostly controlled, and troops remained in the city until the draft could resume in August.[10]

The draft generated waves across society. The mixed response to conscription within Indiana highlighted divisions in both politics and support for the war. Rachel Walters's descriptions in early June gave her husband a glimpse into the home front's reactions. Within her own family, she told of her father, Samuel Ward Jr., becoming an enrolling officer for Pulaski County. In her next letter of June 23, 1863, she relayed the news that Governor Morton sent in troops to the neighboring county of Fulton, where an enrolling officer was beaten to death and draft papers were destroyed. The violence close to home took many forms. In the same letter, she followed with a description of a scene at a local church where one lady attempted to grab the butternut pin, a secessionist emblem, off another.[11] A second lady successfully "snatched" the pin, about which Rachel wrote, "I say bully for her." Though there is no record of her own participation in the fight, Rachel's opinion of the outcome clearly shows her stance on the political divide.

ISAAC WALTERS TO RACHEL J. WALTERS

Camp Near Falmouth VA
January the 6th /63

Dear &much respected Sister

with pleasure I Seat myself in order to answer your letter which
came to hand on the fourth of this month   your letter found me
well & was read with the greatest of pleasure   I was glad to hear of
your good health but was Sorry to hear of Davids Sickness but I hope
he is well before this time[12]_ I hope these few lines may find you &
yours enjoying good health & happiness_John Wirick Said he Saw
David at Indianapolis as he was coming to the regiment   he Said
they ware going to Kentuckey_ that is the last that I heard of him_he
Said David was well when he saw him_I was not Surprised at all to
hear of Moores Death_I expected to hear of it long before this time as I
knew the consumption was preying upon his System for a long time but
I was a little Surprised to hear of the other two mens deaths although
the fatigue of a Soldier is hard to endure   I Supose you have
heared of the battle of Fredricksburg_long before this time the details
of which I cannot give here but I Supose you have alredy had a full
account of the Same   Suffice it to Say that we was badly whipped I
was in the battle &escaped unhurt[13] Our Brigade Saved another Bull
run affair[14]_ you will See an account of it in the papers before long if
you have not alredy_We have had fine weather here this winter until
to day   it is raining & has the appearance of a wet Spell_all is quiet
along the lines except an occational Shot on picket George Storde is
Sick in the hospital   he has the fever_lewey Morway has been Sick
but he is geting better   James McCauley is rather poorly but not
dangerously Sick   all the rest of the boys from that Settlement are
well_Eli has got his discharge[15] & I Supose he is at home before this
time_he Started One week ago today   I Saw him safe on the cars_
he was very weak but I hope he has had the good luck to reach home_I
was glad to See him go although I would like to have his company_I
most heartily excuse you for not writing Sooner_Adieu for the present
Write Soon

from your unworthy friend
Isaac Walters

[*A slip of paper enclosed with the January 6, 1863, letter contains instructions.*]

Rachel

please Seal this volentine up nicely & give it to Sarah gants as I send it expressly for her. pleas do not take any offense by it yourself I merely send it to you So I will know whether She gets it or not tell her it is Something Sent to her by a particular friend, but dont tell her who Sent it

We are all well & I hope you are the Same

Yours with much respect
Isaac Walters[16]

DAVID W. WALTERS TO RACHEL J. WALTERS

Riseingsun Febuary 3d 1863

My dear & much loved companion,

    this morning in answer to your letter that I received last night I would say that I am well hopeing that those few lines may find you enjoying they same blessing   may they pleasant smiles of our heavenly father still continue to rest upon us all & may we ever feel greatful to him for his loveing kindness to ward us in giveing us of they bountys of this earth for they sustinence of those week & frail boddys & more espeshely in giving us health while we ar many miles a part but I trust that they thime is not far distant when this wicked rebellion will come to an end when husband & wife & father & mother can again reunite & enjoy one anothers smiles as they have done in days past   God have mercy on us as a nasion=   but to change they subject it is very cold here at this thime but we have good quarters & get a long fine   they men all except a few is in fine health & good spirits   we drill now every day   twice when they wether will ad mit but it is two cold to do much at this thim

    Our Colonel Quarter master Adjutant & commissary was to se us last week setteing up with they company & to se how we was geting a long   they gave us they prais of all they companys of Haveing they best officers they best conducted company they best arangements in camp they best officers & in fact they best company in evrey respect   this is no gass at all as it was told confidentialy to my friend Louderback by they Quartermaster & he is they man that had ort to no as he has they settleing to do with all the companys in person & it would be no advantage whatever to tell any thing that was not trew

    I am vairy much obliged to you for they money you sent   I needed it vairy much as I was out of evrey thing to rite with   We havent got our pay yet but we are expecting they paymaster every day=   Our captain has resined but his vacancy has not yet bin filled[17]   he was a good man but he had such poore health that his servis was never worth any thing to us   I believe that I have nothing more of interest to rite so I will close

yours as ever

D W Walters[18]

DAVID W. WALTERS TO RACHEL J. WALTERS

Glasgow Ky May 7th 1863

Dear Rachel

Again I am priveleged to pen you a few more loins to in form
you that I am well & hearty= Your very kind & welcom letter is at
hand   did I say letter   I could hardley tell whether it was a
letter or a blank as it was so thin that a part of it I could hardley make
out   I guess that it will all be rite   they mey thime you rite as i
suppose you was out of ink at they thime
       While in camp I can get a plenty of paper but it is vairy high=   I
am sorry to here that .=. that money has bin neglected so long   I
am a frade you will loose it   if you dont need money & cant take
they trouble of going after it I will not send any more   as they old
saying is if it aint worth going after it aint worth having=   think not
hard of me for thus speaking   I only wish you to have that which
I save for you & for you then to use it as you wish=   there is some
ferlowing being done a gain   I am strongly in hopes of geting to
come home after a while=   I would be very glad to se you all once
more & enjoy your pleasent company once more=   trew I would
have no objecsions to your being on picket with me to se & learn some
what of their ways & to be company for me   but that is all as this is
no place for a woman & espeshely as good a one as I have got= (pleas
excuse me & dont think me flattering at all)
       I some thimes wish you could be here to here they Kentuckeyins
talk & obserr they old fashioned women with their strate legs
(excuse) say strate dresses=   I dot suppose that those back woods
Kentucyens ever saw a book or herd of any thing of they kind if they did
they perhaps thot that it was some in provement in hooping tobacco or
whiskey barrels   as they seam to be King & Queen of some of they
parts of this State where I have bin=   if I had thime I would give
you a Short Sketch of they ways & fashions of this country but thime
will not ad mit of it now   I will endeveor to give you some of they
out lines in a future letter=   We have mooved camp a gain we now
have the best Camp that we have had Since in they Servis=   Our
general has come at last=   there has not bin a great eal of showing
done in they last few days in consequince of his new arrangements thill
~~yester~~ [illegible deletion] yesterday morning   a squad of 75 went out

& they report came in this morning that they was skermishing with
they Rebles near Edmonton this is they only skermishing that there has
bin of our forces this week=   We ar to be organised in to they 23d
Armey Corps   I can tell you nothing in regard to our stay   here
they soldier knows but little a bout what a ganerals moovements is
going to be=   but there is one thing sertain if there is any fighting
to be done they soldier has it to do & privates in many respects deserve
more credit than many of their superiors=   So fare you well

yours as ever.
D. W. Walters[19]

RACHEL J. WALTERS TO DAVID W. WALTERS

Starcity Pulaski Co. Ind.
Sunday Morning May 31st 1863

My Dear beloved companion

I this pleasant sabbath morning find myself seated for the purpose of talking to one I [*illegible phrase*] dear through the great medium of pencil and paper. This morning finds me well, and I do hope that these lines may find you enjoying the same good blessing of God. I received your kind and ever welcome letter of May 19th/ 63[20] last wednesday and read it with much interest but I am ashamed to think that I have not answered it, but I hope you will not think hard of me as I had just sent one to you the day before I received yours and I was very busy as we was not through planting corn yet and pap had calculated to plant another small piece yet   but it is so wel that I think perhaps he will give it up   it stormed and hailed here very hard last wednesday and thursday both and it has raind more or less ever since until this morning   it has broke away and has the appearance of some fairer weather   I believe I told you in my last letter that grand pap Fallis[21] was to go and get that money for me and Mrs Sutton come from there yesterday and she said that he told her to tell me that he went to see about it but the man was not at home and the woman would not let him have it but he intended to go back again to see about it. I will now try to give you a few more particulars concerning the death of your dear mother as I have receive a couple of letters one from Mary Washburn and one from Martha[22]   She eat her dinner as usual with the rest of the family and done up the work   she told Emma and Jane[23] to go out and help dady[24] plant corn and about three oclock Emma could come in and help her get supper and when Emma got to the gate she saw her mother lying on our old porch   Emma could not approach her but called her several times but poor mother did not answer her. it was not long till all were brought present by the screams of poor Emma. she was lying on her face with her hand on her head they held an inquest over her the verdict was that her death was caused by a fit of apoplexy all was done that could be done to restore her to life but all in vain   her condition was such that they was obliged to consign her to the tomb in 24 hours after her death   she was buried one week ago to day at three oclock

[*Letter continues on another sheet.*]

Martha stated they intended to send for me but there was a misunderstanding until it was to late. I was very sorry that I could not see her but she is gone from labor to reward and now dear, as we can never more see her any more in this world   let us try to meet her in that blessed world above where partings are no more for we know not the day or the hour that we may be called to another world let us therefore be prepared so that if should fall as suddenly as she did that we may fall with our faces zionward and meet her and all that blood washed throng who had gone up through tribulation and washed their robes and made them white in the blood of the lamb. David I can never go to bed with out thinking of you and wondering if you are on guard and wishing that I could be with you at your post and be company for you in your lonely hours if you want me to send you any more paper or if you cannot get it there as cheap as I can have just let me know

> I will close as ever yours in love,
> Rachel
>
> please write soon and give all the news
>
> [*Another postscript is written on the first sheet.*]
> I understood yesterday that you sent a paper
> to Star city directed to Mary A Ward please
> let me know who you intend it for[25]

Rachel J. Walters to David W. Walters

Star City June 8th 1863

My Dear and much loved companion

   in haste I take up my pen to write you a few lines in answer to your
very kind and welcome letters of which I have received two since I last
wrote to you. you will please excuse me for not writing sooner as I had
some work in hand that had to be done and I could not get time to write
until now, but this morning finds me well and I hope these lines may
find you well Willy is well   he calls himself Willy boy altogether.
I was at meeting yesterday at the miller school house. there was two
united with the church   Mr and Mrs Long and Eliza Nickles was
baptised   we had a very good meeting   I wished you could
have been there   O that I could see you or even know that you had
made that blessed choice and come out on the lords side   it would
rejoice my poor heart O David remember that now is the time to serve
the lord for we know not what day or hour that we may be called away
to another world and let us be prepared to go whenever we are called
for   Mr Dickson said that I must tell you that he wanted to know
~~that~~ whether you was a christian or not   he said he hoped you was
and I hope so to. James Graves told Pap that dady was going to make a
sale and break up house keeping and him and Emma was going to live
at Eli's   Mr Long told me yesterday that he supposed that our dear
brother wesley was dead. he said that he heard that he was wounded
in a battle below Vicksburg[26] and had his leg taken of up in his thigh
and that it had mortified and they did not think that he could live yet I
feel to hope that it is not so for it seems so hard to have to give our dear
brother up. ~~in this~~ I received two Miniatures from you last week   I
think that the one with the hat on is so natural   it looks like you did
when you was at home   at work they are so nice   I would not
part with them for anything, but I must close as pap is about ready to
start to town and I want to send the letter with him

> [*Valediction continues along the side margin.*]
> please excuse my short letter and I will
> try to write again in a few days   please
> excuse my poor writing for my pen is
> very poor   please write soon
> yours in love,
> Rachel[27]

John Wesley Walters to Rachel J. Walters

Memphis Teenn
Ward E Bunk No. 1550
June the 10 /63

Dear Sister

I now as I have the privalige once more, I will try to write you a
few lines this Pleasant morning in answer to your kind Letter which I
Received on the 6th day of June   Your Letter found me wounded,
but I hope when those few ill writen lines comes to hand they will find
you well and all of my friends   we have had Some pretty hard times
Since we left heena[28] we left there on the 13th Day of Aprile and Started
for milligan's Bend[29]   There we got off the Boats and started for
Grand gulf[30]   we got in the Eaveining   At four Oclock we lay
there till the next Day Our gunboat atacked them in the morning about
SunRise   they fought till four oclock p.m. when they Silenced all
the Rebel Batteries   But to which they had case mented, all that
time we were laying on the transports in the River where we could See
Every thing that Passed on after the fite was over, we marched Down
the Leavy about 5 miles and lay there till the next morning. then we got
on the Boats and crossed the River   During the nite the Rebs left
the gulf and Started for Port Gibson   the next morning we Started
in Persuit of them   we marched all Day and only stoped Long
enough to Eat our Supper   then we was ordered to march on and
about 8 oclock AM we heard Some very heavy cannonaidind then our
Boys Raised the yell   it aroused us all, all though we was very tired
and Sleepy, we only got there by day Lite   we only had time to get
our Breakfast when we was ordered in the field   in the morning we
was ordered to Support the Skermishers[31]   I hardly got in the field
till I was hit with a Grape[32] on the finger on my left hand   it did
not cut it off but it nummed my arm considerable, we went into them
like I would into hot cakes and took Revenge   we fought them till
noon when we took one Battery and about 100 prisoners   the next
day the Rebs lef for Jackson and Old U.S. Grant after them Shelling
their Rear all the way   he whiped them and then they Started for
Vicksburg, General Hovie[33] nowing that, he went another Road to Cut
off their Retreat, we found them at a Place called the Champion hills, A
mans name by which the place belonged   he was in the fite and and

got killed, and his company of home pards, as he called them   the
fite commenced on the 16th day of may[34]   Co I was deploid out
as Skermishers   the fite commenced about 10 oclock Am the fite
lasted all day   Gen Hovies Division fought about 40,000 thousand
for about four hours the Rebs say we was badly whiped but we did
not know it   it is true that we was badly cut to Pieces   Our
Regiment went on with about 400 and 60 men and Came out withe
200 and 50 men what doe you think about that   there is where I got
wounded   a musket ball struck me in my rite side just above the
hip   we lay there 3 weeks   then we was [*illegible deletion*] moved
up to memphis at the washington Hospital Ward E   we have six
nice good looking Ladies waiting on the worse cases

    You spoke about Isaac Dunkens Death[35]   I am Very sorrow
to here that   I Suppose you are well   I hope so   You also
Spoke About David   I am glad you you told me where he is   I
have wrote him Aig Long Letter   if he gets it I want you to let me
know what he thought of it   I will close by Saying good by for the
Present   hoping to see you all   Let Arthur[36] Read this as I doe
not feel like Seting up any Longer

Yours truly,
J. W. Walters

Direct to memphis Tenn hospital
Washington ward E

[*Postscript continues on side margin.*]
Write as soon as you get
this   John W.[37]

RACHEL J. WALTERS TO DAVID W. WALTERS

Star City Ind
Sunday June 14th 1863

My Dear Companion

once more I attempt to write you a few lines to let you know that I
am well and I do sincerely hope when these few ill written lines comes
to hand they may find you enjoying the same good blessing of God
for which we ought to be very thankful. I received your ever welcome
letter of June 7th[38] yesterday evening and read with much interest
and O what joy it brought to me   I hardly knew how to contain
my feelings. I truly feel thankful to the god of heaven in that he has
heard and answered my prayers and I hope that he will continue so
to do   O David try in to live faithful and grow in grace and in the
knowledge of the truth as it is christ Jesus our lord that we may meet
our dear mother and friends. friends thats gone before in a better world
above for I believe that she is as an angel watching and waiting to
meet us the banks of sweet deliverance where partings are known no
more   I feel very thankful to Mr Louderback for his information
and satisfaction which them lines gave me.[39] In regard to that money I
do not want you to think that I did not want it for this was not the case.
we had a great deal of sickness here and was so much behind with the
work that we could not well go after it and I was told that they would
not do anything with it until they had further orders. Please do not
think hard of me for so neglecting it   if you think proper to send
any more I will endeavor to do the best I can with it. I wish I could see
you and talk with you I have so many things to tell you that I dare not
write. It has now been almost six months since I saw you and it seems
so long to me. I wish the war was over for I want you to come home so
bad. I hope it will not be long at any rate. they are enrolling the men
here for another draft they enroll all from twenty to forty five years of
age pop is the enrolling officer for Pulaski Co. I do not know how soon
they will draft Mr Washington Taylor is married to Miss Mary Ann
Keys   they was Married last thursday   Willy is well he knows
your likeness when he sees it   he says it is pretty Pa. but I must close
by asking you to remember me at a throne of grace   please write
soon so no more at present   from your affectionate wife

in love
Rachel Walters[40]

RACHEL J. WALTERS TO DAVID W. WALTERS

Star City June 23rd/ 63

My Dear Companion,

I embrace the present opportunity of writing you a few lines to let you know that I am well and I hope that when these lines reaches you they may find you enjoying the same blessing of God   I have not received a letter from you for over a week[41] and I thought as I had an opportunity of ~~writin~~ sending to the office this morning that I would write you a few lines   I received a letter from Wesley last saturday evening dated June 10th   he was then able to set up and write so I am in hopes he will yet recover   he was not wounded in the leg as I had heard but he said he was wounded in the right side just above his hip. He said he had written you a long letter and he wanted me to let him know what you thought of it. he is in the Washington hospital at Memphis[42]   I believe I told you in another letter that they was enrolling the men for another draft   there is so many secesh in fulton Co that some of them refused to be ~~drafted~~ enrolled and they beat one of the enrolling officers almost to death and burned all his papers so the Gov sent on a lot of soldiers to take care of them. Last sunday there was a young lady by the name of Humes wore a butter nut[43] on her shawl to the Presbyterian church and Sarah Campbell tried to take it off of her but she would not let her but Virginia Mcan Snatched it off of her shawl and kept it and would not let her have it   I say bully for her. Willy is still well   they are plowing corn with Kate   she works as well as the rest of the horses but I must close as I have nothing very interesting to write   if I could only see you I could tell you a great many things that I cant write   please excuse all maistakes and write soon

yours in love
Rachel Walters

remember me at a throne of grace/

To David Walters[44]

RACHEL J. WALTERS TO DAVID W. WALTERS

Star City Pulaski Co Ind.
Wednesday June 24th 1863

My Dear Companion

I again seat myself in order to try to write you a few lines in answer to your very kind letter of June 19th[45] this morning and read with much interest your letter found me well and I hope this may find you enjoying the same good blessing of god David it seems to me its possible that I think more of you now than ever I did in my life O David live faithful and grow in grace and in the knowledge of the truth as it is in Christ Jesus our Lord. Yes David I will always remember you at a throne of grace and I hope you will remember me also I also received them tracts they are very nice there was a sabbath school celebration in Star City today. there is to be a union speech there tomorrow evening I expect they will have a great time I do not know whether they will try to enlist any soldiers or not.[46] Willy is well I brought him to Star City with me today and I must hurry home as it is getting late, and I have not much news to write as I just wrote a letter to you yesterday. so I must close and start home I hope you will excuse my short letter and I will try to do better next time please excuse all mistakes well I have just received a letter I must see who it is from well I have read my letter it is from aunt Martha Fallis[47] she says they are all well she says grand pop got that money it is at his house it is safe now in just as good hands as if I had it so no more at present but write soon

yours in love,
Rachel[48]

[DAVID W. WALTERS] TO RACHEL J. WALTERS

[Paper is torn and there is loss of words along the right
margin on the back of this single sheet of paper.]

~~CinC~~ CinCinnatti Ohio
july the 15/ 63
on Board the wren

Dear rachel

i am once more pramitted to writ you a few lines to inform you
of my good holth   you must excuse me for not writeing sooner
as i have not had an opportunity until now   we left glasgow on
the 22 and have not Been in Camp 3 days since most all the time on a
forsed march we got on the cars at lisabeth town Ky[49] and Come up to
louisville   we got there 12 oclock in the night and the next morning
i thought i would wright you a few lines and had a letter half written
when we received marching orders for Cin Ohio i suppose for you
know what its for   its to try to ketch old john[50] i am verry glad we
have left Ky   it is so awful hot   i dont know where we will go
from here nor dont Care   i am verry glad the rebbles is tearing the
free states   let the Cowards suffer a little as well as us   mebby
this will convince them[51]

i will Close By saying good By
[unsigned][52]

~~direc~~ direct to the
5th ind Cavalry Battery[53]
in Care of liut roads[54]

[DAVID W. WALTERS] TO RACHEL J. WALTERS

/63
July the 22
Meiggs Co Ohio
Pomroy town[55]

dear Rachel,

i improve the present by saying that i am well and harty   we had
a fight last sunday with morgan and whipped him so badly   our
loss is about 15 kied wounded and missing   rebble loss 100 killed
and 2200 prisoners   they had a nice position but was to cowardly
to hold it   the most of the fighting was done the artilery so you see
that i had a large hand in it   the first dash the rebbles Captured one
piece of our artilery but in about 20 minutes we recaptured it   we
shel them away from it and when the cavalry saw this ~~they~~ they dashed
across the field with the wind with a yell which almost shook the
earth   we fired 21 rounds from our piece ~~not~~ my position is a ~~post~~
postillion which is the [*illegible deletion*] driver   i am driver on no
2 gun[56]   while the boys wer fireing i sat on my horse eating cakes
and apples   since we have ben in america we have had no use for
a canteen or haversack[57]   i am in Better hope of the war closeing
now than i ever have had before   it seemes to me hat they are about
played out   john mor morgan has but 1500 men left and our forces
are perseuing him   he is in a hard rowfor stumps   we got off
Boat portsmounth and persueed him by land   we Caught him
about 175 miles above Cin Ohio[58] at a place C Called Bovingtons island
where he has going to Cross But Cross the yankees first[59]   Rachel
i still am trying to live a Cristian   i want you to Content your self i
am doing well   i have a nice position in the artilery   no guard
duty at all   the postillion has the easiest Burth in the Service
Rachel i have one thing to toell you which is sad newes   my
Companion is ded his name was Charles groat   he was a kind
friend   he was sick 5 days   he dad with the flucks[60]   poor
fellow   i did not goet to see him at all But i hope to meet him in a

While his regiment closed in on Confederate brigadier general John Hunt Morgan's troops, David W. Walters wrote to his wife, Rachel, on July 22, 1863, with a personal account of his company's pursuit of the raiders. (*National Postal Museum, Smithsonian Institution, 1991.0291.18*)

fairer world than this   i believe i will Close By saying that i have heard from you since the first of july but i suppose it on acount of our traveling   it is about time to go and feed my horses   i have the Best team in the Battery   i dont know where we will go from here

good By for this time
[*unsigned*][61]

this ribon i send you Come out of a dead rebbles pocket[62]

HEADQUARTERS 5TH IND., CAVALRY,
Bardstown, Ky., August 1st. 1863.

Special Order,
No. 1.

1. The town of Bardstown, and Nelson county, is under Martial Law, until further orders from these Headquarters.

2. Lieut. J. G. Rhodes is made Provost Marshal, — he has authority to grant all passes, see that proper police duty is performed in the town during the continuance of martial law, see that the citizens are properly protected in their SOVEREIGN rights, as citizens, and NOT MOLESTED IN ANY WAY.

3. Business of all descriptions, will be continued as though martial law was not in force, unless by special order from these Headquarters.

By order,

T. H. BUTLER,
Lieut. Colonel Commanding Regiment.
JAMES ROBERTS, *Adjutant.*

The command of Fifth Indiana Cavalry issued Special Order 1, which enacted martial law in Bardstown, Kentucky, on August 1, 1863, in support of General Order 120 to protect the area from Confederate skirmishing before the state election. David Walters enclosed the print in his letter of the same date. *(National Postal Museum, Smithsonian Institution, 1991.0291.24)*

David W. Walters to Rachel J. Walters

bardstown Ky
Bardstown Ky 63
august the first

I once more resume the seat of a soldier to inform you of my good health   i am sorry that i could not write sooner But you must excuse me   i will do the verry best i can   this is a rebble town and the are verry ill now   i would have written a louisvelle but we was so verry bussy drawing and exchangeing horses that i haddent time   i now have the 3d pare of horses Since we started after morgin   many fine horses fell as we marched along but never stop   for that we expect to stay here untill after alection and then go to lebnan Ky   This is a verry nice town but rebbles in it[63]   you so say you was surprised to here that i was at Cin[64] But if you had went the trip you would not have been but i am all right now   i had not heard from you for about a month but i trust in the great being that he will tak Care of my little famlly untill my return   morgan Captured our mil and i suppose he got the letter that wrote the 3d of july at tomkinsville   as we Came up from elisabe th th town[65] we saw where he tre / it up[66]

our mail has went on to lebnan lebnan   we laid at pomroy 3 days after the fight then we marched down to gallipolies and there got on boats about 12 above portsmouth   we met the packet Boston   we soon discovered that she was in fire she a tried to run ashore but was unmanageable but the watter was shallow and there was none lost

i believe i will clo Close for the present

Write soon
D.W. Walters[67]

DAVID W. WALTERS TO RACHEL J. WALTERS

63

Aug the 7nth

Camp near lebnan Ky

This morning finds me reasonable well   we arrived here a day or two ago and to my ~~su~~ surprise i found william house here with the rest of the Convolesant soldiers   last night about 12 oclock we received marching orders but was Contremanded this morning   it put us to a good deal of trubble for nothing but we are used to this & how i would like to see you and willy but as i cant i must the the best i Can   i ~~think~~ think when we leave here we will go further south   o rachel take good care of willy   i am sorry to hear of him being sick   i dont think the war Can last much longer and then i Can Come home to stay   i am proud to say that i have helped to do some of the best work that has been done when we started after morgn we turned over our tents and blankets and have none ~~yo~~ yet but the rebbles have none and i Can stand as ~~mu~~ much as any rebble   there was about twenty buildings burned in this town   there was three rebble sitisizins hung here after Morgn passed through   i wish you would tell ~~m~~me what position wesley has   i heard that he ~~and~~ was ordily sergent[68]   the talk is that we will go to mississippi

i belive i will close for the present

write soon

David W

WWW

David[69]

David W. Walters to Rachel J. Walters

Glasgow
the Aug 10[70]

dear rachel

i improve the presant By writeing you a few lines in order to let you Know how i am geting along   i have not been verry well for some time but am all right now   i have just received a letter from eli and he states about isaac   they have had ha a hard a hard old time but our march far exceeds theres   our march was between 1000 and 1500 mles but we had transportation from elisabeth town to louisville and from there to portsmouth ohio and coming back from gallipolies to louisville and the rest of the way   we took it hills over and fences under [illegible deletion] the Bugal has just sounded Boots and saddle[71] and i will has to stop for the present   we are going to Camp [illegible deletion] we have just moved in to Camp   we have a nice camp   i dont know how long we will stay haere but the talk is that we will go further south   it was verry cool laying a out with out any blankets or tents while in ohio we have not got any yet   i believe i Can stand almost anyting   i belive i will close by saying take good care of your self and willy
   write soon

good by   DWW
David Walters[72]

ISAAC WALTERS TO RACHEL J. WALTERS

Fort Schuyler[73] Sept 26th/
63

Dear & much respected Sister

This pleasant afternoon finds me Seated with pen in hand to acknowledge the receipt of your kind & welcom letter which came to hand this morning. your letter found me well & very well contented. I was really glad to hear from you once more as it is a long time Since I received your letter previous to this one when your letter came to hand we was on a march & I had no chance to answer it as there was no mail leaving the Regiment & I had no chance to answer it until we came to N.Y. City   It had been So long Since I had received your letter that I was ashamed to answer it & thought I would wait until you wrote again before I would write. perhaps my letter would have been more acceptable then than now. I cannot Say myself but if So I hope you will look over it & forgive me this time as I believe it is the first offense & one of not very great magnitude any way. we are Stationed here in the fort doing garrison duty.[74] we have a very pleasant & a healthy place   Our guard duty is pretty heavy but it is a happy Change for us & every thing goes off well the health of the Regiment is good & we are all in fine Spirits.

I am glad to hear that David had a hand in the fracus with morgans forces. I think it is a great pity they did not kill him instead of capturing him   I think all Such fellows as him ought to be out of the way. I wonder how David likes the Service by this time. I am glad to hear that he is well again   health is a great blessing any where but it is a greater one in the army than any place else for it is a very poor place for a Sick man   any person not having a good Constitution had better stay out of the army. you mentioned [*illegible deletion*] Isaac Dunkan in your letter Saying he used to be acquainted with me. I think his acquaintance with me was very Slight for I dont Remember of ever Seeing him   I didnt know there was Such a man in the

regiment   I think he must have been mistaken in the person. There
was a man in our Company by the name of Richard Dunkan   he
was discharged last Summer Soon after the Bull Run Battle   he is
the only Dunkan that I ever knew in the regiment   I asked John
Wirick about it & he Says he knew him So we know he once belonged
to the Regiment I close for the present From your well wishing Friend
until Death Direct to Fort Schuyler New York Harbor

> Write Soon
> Isaac Walters[75]

[ISAAC WALTERS] TO [RACHEL J. WALTERS]

[*Front of letter remnant.*]
Virginia Oct 25th /63
Dear Sister [*loss*]

[*Back of letter remnant.*]
Catlet Station on the Rail Road. The rebels made a Raid in the rear of
the army before we [*loss*][76]

DAVID W. WALTERS TO RACHEL J. WALTERS

Sunday 25 63 east tenn
October the Camp near
jonesburry[77]

dear rachel

    i once more take the presant opportunity of writing you a few lines to inform you of my good health   i have written two letters and reseived non answer but i do trust in that great Being i have been in several Battles since i last wrote but have escaped unharmed   i want ly to hear from you so bad   how i would like to bee with you   I direct to Knoxville 5th Cavalry Company[78]   i as i am back to the Company again

write soon
D. W. Walters[79]

David Walters folded this paper written with romantic lines to his wife, Rachel, signed the reverse with their initials, and enclosed it with his November 4, 1863, letter. (*National Postal Museum, Smithsonian Institution, 1991.0291.31.2*)

DAVID W. WALTERS TO RACHEL J. WALTERS

November the 4/ 63[80]

dear Rachel,

it is with much respect that i take this presant opportunity of writeing to you   i am well at presant hopeing this will find you the same   i am driveing for teem at present   john auter is well he belongs to Co. a   the health fo the rigt is verry good   we muster about 600 men   the reason why i am driveing team is because i was detailed   rachel i will try and Come home this winter do rest Contented   i dont expect i would know nor i expect you are a perfect hatchet face   rachel dont forget to prey for me   tell the Christian friends to & rachel i think of the often   i received a letter from arthur the other day but i will not answer it now   i am verry fat   i weigh 195 lBs although i have seen some verry hard times   if it had not been the Corn and Apples we have suffered verry much   Col grayham[81] says that we have done more duty ~~than~~ than any other two regt in the same time   i will close for the presant by saying direct to Co. I Co i

David W. Walters
of the 5 ind Cav

[*illegible deletion*]
4th brigade 4 of the
9th division
23 army
Corps[82]

David W. Walters 5th ind
Cav
4th brigade
9th devision
twenty third army
Corps

[*Front of a slip of paper enclosed with the November
4, 1863, letter contains a verse.*]

my love for you you here unfold
tis just like this ring of gold
my love for you Can never end
my ever true and perfect friend
let us ever watch and pray and love
rejoiceing every day

[*Back of the slip of paper is signed.*]
D W W
R J W[83]

JOHN WESLEY WALTERS TO RACHEL J. WALTERS

Head Quarters
November 8 1863
Depot Guards[84]

Dear Sister

I this sabath after noon Sit in order to write to you to let you know
where I am and how I get along. I hope when those few ill written
lines comes to hand they will find you all well and doing well. I am
well at the present and I Enjoy my Self as well as any of the rest of the
Soldiers that is in the field   I have had fine times Since I Came here.
I am now at this Depo guarding trains that rims from here to Grand
Junction and back again   I am off of duty one day and on two   it
was my luck to come of today and I thought I would write and let you
know where I was So you would know where I was and when you
write   I want you to let me know where David is and what he is a
doing   I have not Known where he is nor I have not heard where
he is since I came here   I have written two letters Since I came here
and I have not heard from him yet   when you write to him tell him
to write to me and if he dont answer my letters David not try to let
him know anything about me   if he dont think enough of me to
write to me I dont think it worth while to spent ink and paper to write
to him   I thought it was his duty to answer all of my letters, and I
would his but it Seems as if he dont care   it may bee that he has not
got the letters   tell him to let me know where to direct to and I will
answer imediately   I am well pleased with my burth   it is far
better than to bee to my regiment marching Every day and Sometimes
all nite   here we have our bunks to lay in and good lite Bakers bred
to Eat and our regular meals Every day   we have two men imploid
to doe our cooking and they doe nothing Else   we will draw our
pay here and our Clothing first the same as if we was in the regiment.
this is what our Old Captain says that is in Charge of us and if that bee
the case we will have some fine times. I think I will stay here all winter
if nothing happens.[85] tell Arthur I want him to write to me as Soon as
you get this and I will answer all his letters promptly, and I want him
to Doe the same. I suppose you have heard from Isaac Since I left and
if you have I want you to let me know where [illegible deletion] he is
and what he is doing   I wrote to him but I have not Received any

answer yet. but I am looking for a letter from him Every day but I dont
know when I will get one   I hope he is well and well sadisfied for
as long as we keep well we ought to bee sadisfied where Ever we may
bee   all I wish is that if I only keep well till my time is out and then
I will wrest the next three years to Come   I have done my duty like
aman   So far and I can doe it alittle while longer   it will not bee
long till my time is out and then I will Bee free once more. well Rachel I
want you to answer this as Soon as you get this and dont delay

> yours truly
> J.W. Walters
> [*illegible words*]
>
> Mrs. Rachel J. Walters
>
> Direct to Memphis Tenn
>
> Give my love to all
> Good by but not
> forever
> Your True
> Brother in marriage
>
> [*Postscript continues on side margin.*]
> As I have no Stamps I will have
> to Send this without paying for
> it[86]   I hope you will excuse
> me for this time   I want you to
> Excuse all Poor writing and poor
> Spellings[87]

Isaac Walters to Rachel J. Walters

Station V.A.
Camp Near Brandy[88]
Nov 24th /63

Dear Sister,

    with pleasure I take up my pen in order to answer your kind epistle
which came to hand about one week ago. but I could not answer it any
sooner as I had no Ink nor paper & could not get any as there were no
Sutlers[89] to be found with the Army. but now I have obtained both
Ink & paper & proceed to answer your letter which found me well
& was gladly received & read with much pleasure. I was glad to hear
that you Still enjoy good health & hope it may Still be extended unto
you in your lonely & Sad hours for I have no doubt but what you have
Some lonesome hours. I am also glad to hear that Willy is well how I
would like to See him   I hope you all may be permitted to enjoy
good health which is one of the greatest blessings that can be bestowed
upon us. we are Stationed about Six miles from Culpeper between the
Rhappahonnock & the Rhapidan Rivers. we have been here two weeks
yesterday   we crossed the Rhappahannock two weeks ago last
Saturday   we had quite a brisk fight at the river but Succeeded in
dislodging the Enemy & driving him across the Rhapidan a distance of
about 20 miles[90]
    This morning we was ordered to march again & struck tents but
before we got Started it began to rain & looked as if we were going to
have a wet time so the order was Countermanded and we was ordered
to pitch tents again. Where we are going I am not able to tell. but I
think your will hear of another battle Soon again in the Army of the
Potomac   I got a letter from Wesley   lately he is well & at
Memphis Tenn. I now belong to the Pioneer Corps[91] & dont expect to
fight much more for they are Generally to the rear in time of action. I
have nothing of importance to write So I will close by Saying Good bye
for the present

Write Soon
Isaac[92]

ISAAC WALTERS TO RACHEL J. WALTERS

Camp Near Brandy Station Virginia Dec. 16th /63

Much Respected Sister

   Your Truly welcome letter came to hand in due time & found me well & now I compose myself in order to reply hoping when these lines reach you they may find you & yours enjoying good health and happiness. I am glad Still to hear of your good health & you Said you had been butchering   how I would liked to been there. I always like to be around about Such times   they Generally have a merry time & plenty to eat & that is what makes a person feel happy. I always feel good when my belly is full (if you will allow me the expression)   I am glad to hear you have had Such a fine fall & winter there So far. I hope you have enjoyed your Selves well. I wish I could have been there to have Some of your Sports with you. but I feel glad the is fast approaching that we can have this glorious privilege if God is willing we Should. what a happy thought to be free once more placed among your friends dear to you where you can have free exercise of your own mind. free to do & act once more   this is a very happy thought & one of great Importance to the Soldier. I think if I am once free I always will remain So. They are now Granting Furloughs to Soldiers in this Army   one man in every Company that has proven himself to be a good & brave Soldier can get a Furlough for 15 days   Sergt Morgan was the man from our Company   he Started for home this morning with nine others from the Regiment   they are now on their way with happy hearts   I hope they may have a good time & a Safe journey as for myself I think I can Stand it until my time is out   I have Stood it over two years & I think I can Stand it Six or Seven months longer   I have never asked for a furlough yet nor I dont expect to although I had a great notion of it twice Since I have been in the Service but Something or other always occured to prevent me from asking. now I have declined the intention entirely as I think the cost would overrun the profits as my time is So near out. we have had very nice weather all along until yesterday   it clouded up & last knight it rained all knight & is raining all day to day. This is a very gloomy disagreeable day   I think our winter is about to Set in from all appearance.

In the recent engagement our Regiment lost Eleven wounded. none killed. One wounded in Co. F   he was a Corporal   his name is Charles Goodair   he was wounded through the left wrist both bones being fractured & it is Sad his hand has Since been Amputated   Our Regiment was extremely lucky this time & I am very glad of it. it is not often the case with us. I under Stand the Army is going to fall back across the Rhappahannock River to winter. there is not a sufficient quantity of timber here to winter the Army here So we will have to go Some place or other & I under Stand there is where we are going   I think the move will be made as Soon as the roads will admit of it So we can get into winter quarters. I got a letter from Wesley the Same time I got yours. He was complaining Some withe the Rhumatism. he was well otherwise   he is Still at Charleston Depo[93] Memphis Tenn   As I have nothing of Importance or perhaps nothing that will Interest you, I will close for the present hoping to get a Speedy reply

Yours as Ever with high regards.
Isaac Walters[94]

Star City Pulaski Co Ind
Tuesday evening December 22d/63

Kind and affectionate companion, once more I attempt to address you by the silent language of the pen. This evening finds me well and I hope that these lines may find you enjoying the same blessing of God. It is now almost three weeks since I have received a letter from you and it is almost two months since that was written and oh how long it seems to me not to hear from you and if I could hear from you as often as I used to it would not seem quite so hard. It is just one year ago to day since I last saw you and oh what a long year it has seemed to what the last two before it did. Wednesday Dec 23

Dear David I again seat myself to try to finish my letter as I did not get to finish it last night, and Phebe come to pass and wanted me to come to Star City with her and I had not time to finish it so I thought that I would bring it to Clems.

There is quite an excitement here about the draft there has enough enlisted to fill the quota and there was a meeting to night to to pay them their bounty this township gives so dollars bounty to each volunteers. Phebe is staying with aunt Julias yet she send you her best respects and well wishes

The letter from Rachel to her husband, David W. Walters, on December 22, 1863, expressed her patriotic sentiments. It is the only missive in this collection with an illustration drawn by the sender. (*National Postal Museum, Smithsonian Institution, 1991.0291.53*)

Rachel J. Walters to David W. Walters

Star City Pulaski Co Ind
Tuesday evening December 22nd/63

Kind and affectionate companion,

once more I attempt to address you by the silent language of the pen. This evening finds me well and I hope that these lines may find you enjoying the same blessing of God. It is now almost three weeks since I have received a letter from you and it is almost two months since that was written and oh how long it seems to me not to hear from you If if I could hear from you as often as I used to it would not seem quite so hard. It is just one year ago today since I last saw you and oh what a long year it has seemed to what the last two before it did.[95]

[*Letter continues on the next day and with a different ink.*]

Wednesday Dec. 23

Dear David

I again seat myself to try to finish my letter as I did not get to finish it last night and Phebe came to paps and wanted me to come to Star City with her and I had not time to finish it so I thought that I would bring it to Clems.

There is quite an excitement here about the draft   there has enough enlisted to fill the quota and there is a meeting to night to pay them their bounty   this township gives 50 dollars bounty to each volunteers. Phebe is staying with aunt Julias yet she send you her best respects and well wishes

I believe I will close for the present as it is getting late and I must hurry home as I want to go to the speaking to night   please excuse all mistakes and my poor writing for I am in a hurry please excuse all write as soon as you get this for I do want to hear from you so bad this is the third letter that I have written since I received one[96] so no more at present

but I close as ever yours in love,
Rachel J. Walters[97]

NOTES

1. Indiana Infantry, *History of the Forty-Sixth Regiment*, 210.
2. McPherson, *Battle Cry of Freedom*, 636–637.
3. Nation and Towne, *Indiana's War*, 146–148.
4. McPherson, *Battle Cry of Freedom*, 293.
5. McPherson, *Battle Cry of Freedom*, 284–297.
6. "Martial Law in Kentucky."
7. The Chancellorsville Campaign saw the 133,000 men of the Union army under General Joseph Hooker moving against 61,000 men under Confederate general Robert E. Lee across the Rapidan River in Virginia in an attempt to destroy Lee's army and capture Richmond. Through a series of bold maneuvers, including a flank attack on the Union position, Lee was able to overcome the difference in manpower and defeat Hooker's advance at the Battle of Chancellorsville, though at the cost of 20 percent of the Confederate army (Gallagher, *Chancellorsville*, ix–xiii). The Twentieth Indiana was a part of Brigadier General David B. Birney's division, and took part in the capture of the Twenty-Third Georgia during the initial stages of the battle before being forced to retreat after the Union defeat (Bohannon, "Disgraced and Ruined," 207).
8. Rosiecki, "Gettysburg in My Hometown." The Gettysburg Campaign involved the Army of Northern Virginia, under the command of Confederate general Robert E. Lee, moving north from Virginia, through Maryland, and into Pennsylvania. Lee hoped to gather supplies for the army, cause panic in the North, and possibly bring about an end to the war if the Union army could be defeated. The two armies clashed for three days from July 1 to July 3, 1863, in and around the town of Gettysburg, Pennsylvania, resulting in a crushing Confederate defeat and over fifty thousand combined casualties (Guelzo, *Gettysburg*, 33–34).
9. McPherson, *Battle Cry of Freedom*, 601–605.
10. McPherson, *Battle Cry of Freedom*, 608–611.
11. A similar incident involving a butternut emblem at the Terre Haute Female Academy is cited in Thomas E. Rodgers's "Hoosier Women and the Civil War Home Front" as an example of how "the participation of women in public political activities expanded dramatically during the war" (page 118).
12. David Walters received a furlough on November 24, 1862, at the recommendation of A. C. Fosdick, surgeon of the Fifth Indiana Cavalry. The furlough permitted six days of absence from Camp Carrington due to the loss of his voice as a consequence of having had measles at some point in his life, which was described in the disability certificate as "he is suffering from aphonia as a sequela of measles, having been indisposed for 2 weeks without any apparent improvement" (Furlough and Certificate of Disability, David W. Walters, Catalog Num-

ber M-11136, Division of Medicine and Science, National Museum of American History, Smithsonian Institution).

13. Isaac Walters's choice to not include details about the Battle of Fredericksburg was a personal preference since officials did not censor civilian or military letters except for prisoner-of-war mail. The battle took place in and around the city of Fredericksburg, Virginia, from December 11 to 15, 1862. On December 13, Union forces repeatedly attacked across open ground in front of Confederate forces occupying the high ground just beyond the city, resulting in one of the worst defeats of the war and almost thirteen thousand Union casualties compared to five thousand Confederate casualties (McPherson, *Battle Cry of Freedom*, 570–572). After suffering these heavy losses, the Union army retreated and ended fighting for the winter.

14. Both the First and Second Battles of Bull Run (Manassas) ended in publicly and politically embarrassing defeats for Union forces. Isaac Walters's Twentieth Indiana fought in the Second Battle, August 28–30, 1862.

15. Eli Walters received a disability discharge from Company F, Twentieth Indiana in December 1862 for rheumatism (compiled military service record, Eli Walters, Pvt., Co. F, 20 Ind. Inf.; Civil War, RG 94; NA-Washington).

16. The envelope (1991.0291.81) for this letter (1991.0291.79) and enclosed note (1991.0291.80) was postmarked "[OL]D POINT COMFORT / [V]A / FEB 14" over a three-cent George Washington stamp in the lower left corner. It was addressed "Mrs. Rachel. J. Walters / Royal. Center / Cass. Co / Ind." The pencil notation "from Isaac, with a valentine" was added, likely by a family member, after the letter was received and before it was donated to the museum. The letter was written on blue colored stationery embossed with an eagle and shield, and the enclosed note is on cream-colored stationery with blue lines and embossed with a horse set above a crown.

17. Unlike soldiers, officers had the ability to resign their commissions and return home during the Civil War.

18. The handwriting of this letter has characteristics similar to the May 7, 1863, letter (1991.0291.14) but differs from most of the other handwriting in the letters sent by David Walters. The envelope (1991.0291.13) for this letter (1991.0291.12) was addressed "Mrs David W Walters / Starcity Post / Pulaski Co / Ind." It has a cancelled three-cent George Washington stamp in the upper left corner. It was postmarked in the lower right corner "RISING SUN / FEB 3," and the pencil notation "1863" was added to the postmark, likely by a family member, after the letter was received and before it was donated to the museum. Similarly, a blue ink notation was added later in the lower left corner. The letter was written on stationery embossed with a crown set above a shield.

19. The handwriting in this letter has characteristics similar to the February 3, 1863, letter (1991.0291.12) but differs from most of the other handwriting

in the letters sent by David Walters. The envelope (1991.0291.15) for this letter (1991.0291.14) was postmarked "SOMERSET / K.Y. / MAY 8" over a three-cent George Washington stamp. It was addressed "Mrs. D. W / Walters / Starcity Ind." The letter was written on two sheets of stationery, the first of which has a printed illustration of Union ships bombarding Fort Jackson, New Orleans, Louisiana, with the caption, "Great Naval Engagement Off Fort Jackson."

20. The referenced letter, dated May 19, is not in the collection.

21. William Fallis, maternal grandfather of Rachel J. (Ward) Walters.

22. The name Martha likely refers to an older sister of David W. Walters.

23. The names Emma and Jane likely refer to David W. Walters's younger sisters Emmaline Grace and Hannah Jane.

24. Rachel J. (Ward) Walters referred to her father-in-law, John Walters, as "dady."

25. Rachel Walters requested clarification. It seems doubtful the paper was sent to her younger sister Mary J., who was about thirteen years old at the time of this letter. The letter (1991.0291.44.1 and 1991.0291.44.2) was written in pencil on two sheets of blue-lined paper. A matching envelope has not been identified.

26. This news came in the middle of the siege of Vicksburg, May 18 to July 4, 1863.

27. The letter (1991.0291.47) was written on blue-lined stationery embossed with a paper manufacturer's mark. A matching envelope has not been identified.

28. Helena, Arkansas.

29. Milliken's Bend is an area fifteen miles north of Vicksburg, Mississippi.

30. The town of Grand Gulf, Mississippi, was fortified by Confederate forces to prevent Union ships from going up the Mississippi River.

31. Skirmishers were soldiers sent out in front of the main battle line to help locate the enemy.

32. Grapeshot was a type of artillery round that was used effectively against large infantry formations during the Civil War. Consisting of numerous small lead or iron balls instead of one large projectile, grapeshot would be fired at short to medium ranges. The grapeshot spread out once it was fired from a cannon, enabling an artillery piece to inflict multiple casualties with a single firing.

33. Brigadier General Alvin P. Hovey was the commander of the Twelfth Division of the XIII Corps of the Union Army of the Tennessee.

34. The "fite," or fight, that John Wesley Walters described was the Battle of Champion Hill, May 16, 1863. Following the capture of Jackson, Mississippi, Union forces under the command of Ulysses S. Grant encountered Confederate forces commanded by John C. Pemberton on May 16. After intense fighting on and around Champion Hill, Pemberton and his command retreated back into Vicksburg, Mississippi, to protect the city. This retreat allowed Grant to

surround the city and besiege it and Pemberton's troops (Ballard, *Vicksburg*, 282–308).

35. Isaac Dunkin was Rachel J. (Ward) Walters's brother-in-law, married to Phebe A. (Ward) Dunkin. He served with Company D, Twentieth Indiana Infantry, and died on April 24, 1863, shortly after he and Phebe had married on March 6, 1863.

36. This may refer to Arthur M. Ward, younger brother of Rachel J. (Ward) Walters.

37. The letter (1991.0291.74) was written on blue-lined stationery embossed "Greylock." A matching envelope has not been identified.

38. The referenced letter, dated June 7, is not in the collection.

39. The referenced letter from Mr. Louderback is not in the collection.

40. The letter (1991.0291.48) was written on blue-lined stationery embossed "Enterprise Mill." A matching envelope has not been identified.

41. The previous letter by David Walters in the collection dates from May 7 (1991.0291.14); Rachel Walters's reference is likely to a letter not in the collection.

42. John Wesley Walters wrote of this news in his letter of June 10, 1863 (1991.0291.74).

43. Butternut-colored cloth was often used by the Confederacy for military uniforms. It became an unofficial symbol of the Confederacy and was used as a symbol by northern Democrats who opposed the war. Jennifer Weber explains in *Copperheads* that "dissenters in the lower Midwest were also known as 'Butternuts' because of their Southern roots (butternut being the color of their homespun clothes and therefore a term sometimes used to describe impoverished solders)" (page 3).

44. The envelope (1991.0291.50) for this letter (1991.0291.49) has the postmark "STAR CITY / IND. / JUN 23" in the upper left corner and a cancelled three-cent George Washington stamp placed on its side on the upper right corner. It was addressed "David W. Walters 5th / cavalry regiment of Ind / volunteers Co I / Glascow / Kentucky." The letter was written on blue-lined paper.

45. The referenced letter, dated June 19, is not in the collection.

46. Public speeches to encourage support on the home front typically occurred around recruiting efforts and holidays like the Fourth of July.

47. Martha Fallis, younger sister of Sarah Ann (Fallis) Ward, mother of Rachel J. (Ward) Walters.

48. The envelope (1991.0291.52) for this letter (1991.0291.51) has the postmark "STAR C[ITY] / IND. / JUN 25" in the upper left corner and a cancelled three-cent George Washington stamp in the upper right corner. It was addressed "David W. Walters 5th / cavalry regiment of Ind / volunteers Co I. / Glascow

/ Kentucky." The letter was written on blue-lined stationery embossed with a paper manufacturer's mark.

49. Elizabethtown, Kentucky.

50. This referred to "Morgan's Raid," a Confederate cavalry raid led by Brigadier General John Hunt Morgan that started in Tennessee and went through Kentucky, Indiana, and Ohio. The raid lasted from June 11 to July 26, 1863, when Morgan was captured by Union troops.

51. David Walters used the word *free* to describe Kentucky, which remained neutral in the Civil War.

52. The unsigned letter (1991.0291.16) and envelope (1991.0291.17) are in handwriting similar to several others sent by David Walters. The letter is written on a half sheet of stationery. The envelope was postmarked "CINCINNATI / O / JUL 15" over a three-cent George Washington stamp placed in the upper left corner. It was addressed "Mrs. D. W. Walters / Starcity pulaskii / Co ind." Pencil notations "from David" and "1863" were added, likely by a family member, after the letter was received and before it was donated to the museum.

53. David Walters was most likely assigned to an artillery battery within the Fifth Indiana Cavalry.

54. Lieutenant John G. Rhodes of Pierceville, Indiana, served with Company H and was eventually promoted to the rank of captain. From the reference to how to address future mail to the Fifth Indiana Cavalry, Rhodes was handling the mail at the time of this letter.

55. Pomeroy, Ohio.

56. The driver of the gun led the horse team that pulled the gun into position and while traveling.

57. David Walters used the word *america* to describe being in the Union state of Ohio as opposed to the neutral border state of Kentucky, where the regiment had been pursuing Confederate cavalry in Morgan's Raid.

58. Cincinnati, Ohio.

59. The Battle of Buffington Island, fought on July 19, 1863, was one of the final battles of Morgan's Raid, leading to the capture of a large portion of John Hunt Morgan's troops.

60. *Flux* was a period term for dysentery.

61. The unsigned letter (1991.0291.18) and envelope (1991.0291.21) are in handwriting similar to several others by David Walters. The envelope was printed with three-cent postage. It is postmarked "POMERO[Y] / OHIO / JUL 23" in the lower right corner. It was addressed to "Mrs. D. W. Walters / Starcity Pulaski / Co Ind." Written perpendicular to the address by a different hand in pencil is "hearts from dead rebel says he is a Christian." It is unknown who wrote that note on the envelope and to what it referred, perhaps it was the enclosed paper hearts (1991.0291.19). Another pencil notation, "also her letter June 8, '63,"

in a third handwriting was added, likely by a family member, after the letter was received and before it was donated to the museum. The letter was written on stationery embossed with a crown.

62. This postscript on the left edge of the first page runs perpendicular to the main text. There is not a ribbon in this collection; however, there are two keepsakes associated with the letter. One enclosure (1991.0291.19) is made of white and green papers woven together into two connected hearts. "Our hearts" is written in pencil on the white heart. The second keepsake (1991.0291.20) is a rectangular piece of lined paper with an ornamental design drawn in blue ink. It is unknown who created these pieces, and it cannot be confirmed if these were originally enclosed with the July 22, 1863, letter.

63. Enclosed with the letter was a document (1991.0291.24) with printed military orders issued by David Walter's regiment:

HEADQUARTERS 5TH IND., CAVALRY.
Bardstown, Ky., August 1st. 1863.

Special Order
No. 1.

The town of Bardstown, and Nelson county, is under Martial Law, until further orders from these Headquarters.

Lieut. J. G. Rhodes is made Provost Marshal, – he as authority to grant all passes, see that proper police duty is performed in the town during the continuance of martial law, see that the citizens are properly protected in their SOVEREIGN rights, as citizens, and NOT MOLESTED IN ANY WAY.

Business of all descriptions, will be continued as though martial law was not in force, unless by special order from these Headquarters.

By order,
T. H. BUTLER
Lieut. Colonel Commanding Regiment.
JAMES ROBERTS, *Adjutant.*

64. Cincinnati, Ohio.

65. Elizabethtown, Kentucky.

66. David Walters's description of the taking of the regiment's mail ("mil"), which was torn apart ("tre / it up") by Morgan's troops, aligned with a pattern of property theft and destruction during these raids (National Park Service, "Morgan's Raid," 26, 38, 53).

67. The envelope (1991.0291.23) for this letter (1991.0291.22) has a cancelled three-cent George Washington stamp in the upper right corner and was postmarked "B[ARDST]OWN / KY / AUG 3" in the upper left corner. It was ad-

dressed "Mrs. D. W. Walters / Starcity Pulaski / Co Ind." The letter was written on stationery embossed with a paper manufacturer's mark.

68. An orderly sergeant, also known as first sergeant, was a noncommissioned officer rank that included the duties of helping distribute orders from upper ranks to privates.

69. The envelope (1991.0291.26) for this letter (1991.0291.25) was postmarked "LEBANON / KY / AUG 8," and a "Due 6" mark is written for the three-cent penalty for no prepayment of the three-cent postage. Official regulations allowed military personnel to send mail without penalty for not prepaying postage if properly endorsed as "soldier's letter." This envelope was addressed "Mrs. D. W. Walters / Star City, Pulaski / Co ind." The letter was written on stationery embossed with a paper manufacturer's mark.

70. Although no year is written on the letter, the paired envelope is postmarked "[18]63," and military records of the Fifth Indiana Cavalry show that the unit was in the vicinity of the places described in the letter during the summer of 1863.

71. The "boots and saddle" bugle call was used by the cavalry to alert soldiers to mount their horses and line up in preparation for movement.

72. The envelope (1991.0291.28) for this letter (1991.0291.27) was postmarked "GLASGOW / KY / AUG 12 [18]63" to the left of a cancelled three-cent George Washington stamp. It was addressed "Mrs. d. w. Walters / Star City Pulaski / Co ind." A notation, "from David," was added, likely by a family member, after the letter was received and before it was donated to the museum. The letter was written on stationery embossed with a paper manufacturer's mark.

73. The construction of Fort Schuyler, Bronx, New York, predated the Civil War, and, at the time of this letter, the fort was garrisoned and in use to hold prisoners of war.

74. Garrison duty consisted of troops occupying a position, such as a fort, where they served as a lookout and defensive force in case of movement by the enemy against the position.

75. The envelope (1991.0291.83) for this letter (1991.0291.82) was postmarked "[illegible] ORT [illegible]" over a three-cent George Washington stamp placed in the upper left corner. It was addressed "Mrs. Rachel. J. Walters / Star City / Pulaski Co. / Ind." A notation, "Sept 26, '63, from Isaac," was added, likely by a family member, after the letter was received and before it was donated to the museum. The letter was written on stationery embossed with a paper manufacturer's mark.

76. Remnant of blue-lined stationery, with an embossed paper manufacturer's mark, only has a few lines of writing remaining on the front and back of this torn letter (1991.0291.155.2). The handwriting is like that of Isaac Walters. Records of his regiment would place him in Virginia on the date of the letter,

and the mail for Union troops in that area can be found with a postmark from Washington, DC, like the postmark "[WASHIN]GTON / [D].C. / O[CT 2]9 / 1863" on the envelope (1991.0291.155) that has a three-cent George Washington stamp in the upper left corner. The envelope was addressed "Rachel. J. Walters / Star City / Pulaski Co. / Ind."

77. Jonesborough, Tennessee.

78. David Walters asked his wife, Rachel, to direct his mail to Knoxville, Tennessee, as the Fifth Indiana was participating in the Knoxville Campaign. Beginning in late August 1863, in an effort to protect Unionists in East Tennessee and ensure control of the area, General Ambrose Burnside led Union troops to occupy the area and capture Knoxville, which was accomplished without meeting resistance. Confederate general James Longstreet moved two divisions under his command in November to try to recapture the city, and a siege ensued. Union forces had successfully held out when the campaign effectively ended in December following the Confederate losses at the Battles for Chattanooga (November 23–25, 1863). The taking of Knoxville and eastern Tennessee helped secure the area for further actions by Union forces deep into the territory of the Confederacy.

79. The envelope (1991.0291.30) for this letter (1991.0291.29) has a cancelled three-cent George Washington stamp. It was addressed "Mrs D W Walters / Starcity / Pulaski Co / Ind." The pencil notation "1863" was added, likely by a family member, after the letter was received and before it was donated to the museum. The letter was written in pencil.

80. The Fifth Indiana Cavalry was likely in eastern Tennessee when David Walters wrote this letter. The letter is not indicated on the map of David's correspondence because of the imprecise location.

81. Colonel Felix W. Graham, of Clermont, Indiana, resigned from the Fifth Indiana Cavalry on December 15, 1863.

82. The XXIII Corps, known as the Army of the Ohio, was commanded by Major General John Schofield. The Fourth Division, which was the cavalry division, was commanded by Major General George Stoneman.

83. The letter (1991.0291.31.1) and enclosed verse (1991.0291.31.2) are on two pieces of plain paper. A matching envelope has not been identified.

84. In Isaac Walters's December 16, 1863, letter, he cited correspondence received from John Wesley Walters while John Wesley was stationed at the depot for the Memphis and Charleston Railroad, located in Memphis, Tennessee.

85. Compared to being in the field, John Wesley Walters's description of conditions while guarding trains at a depot records a sense of relative comfort, from his "burth," or berth, to the fresh-baked bread, which was a welcome change from sleeping on the ground and eating the hardtack biscuits that were issued to soldiers during campaigns. While in Memphis, Tennessee, he was detached

from serving in his regiment after he was wounded at the Battle of Champion Hill and given guard duty as an easier assignment.

86. Prepayment of domestic US postage using stamps was required as of 1856. However, in July 1861, Congress enacted an exemption for Union military personnel and allowed mail endorsed "soldier's letter" to be sent postage due. After writing this postscript, John Wesley Walters procured postage as evidenced by the stamp on his envelope cancelled in Memphis on November 9, and he did not burden his sister-in-law with the cost of receiving a letter without prepaid postage.

87. The envelope (1991.0291.107) for this letter (1991.0291.106) was postmarked "MEMPHIS / TEN[illegible] / NOV 9" over a three-cent George Washington stamp. It was addressed "Mrs Rachel. J. Walters / Star City / Pulaski Co / Indiana." The letter was written on blue-lined stationery embossed with a paper manufacturer's mark.

88. Brandy Station, Virginia.

89. Sutlers were civilians who were appointed by the US Army to follow the soldiers and sell food and goods that were not issued, such as ink, stationery, stamps, and tobacco.

90. The Battle of Rappahannock Station took place on November 7, 1863.

91. The Pioneer Corps was a group of soldiers tasked with performing construction, such as clearing roads and building bridges, to support the army.

92. The envelope (1991.0291.85) for this letter (1991.0291.84) was postmarked "[WASH]INGTON / NOV 26 / 63" over a three-cent George Washington stamp. It was addressed "Rachel. J. Walters / Star. City / Pulaski. Co. / Ind." The letter was written on blue-lined stationery.

93. John Wesley Walters described his experiences at the depot for the Memphis and Charleston Railroad, located in Memphis, Tennessee, in his November 8, 1863, letter (1991.0291.106) to Rachel Walters.

94. The envelope (1991.0291.87) for this letter (1991.0291.86) was postmarked "WAS[HING]TON / DC / DEC 26 / 63" over a three-cent George Washington stamp. It was addressed "Mrs. Rachel. J. Walters / Star. City. Pulaski Co. Ind." The letter was written on blue-lined stationery embossed with a crown over a shield.

95. A visit between David and Rachel Walters on December 22, 1862, was not recorded in other letters in the collection. A record of being absent with leave exists for November 1862, but there is no record of a December 1862 furlough in David's military service records (compiled military service record, David W. Walters, Pvt., Co. I, 5 Ind. Cav.; Civil War, RG 94; NA-Washington).

96. David Walters's letter (1991.0291.31) dated November 4, 1863, was the closest to the date of this message, but there are no letters in the collection by Rachel Walters in the interim.

97. The blue-lined stationery has a patriotic drawing in the upper left corner featuring six stars and a US flag with the caption "Union Forever" in blue ink that matches the December 22 portion of the letter (1991.0291.53). The December 23 portion was written in brown ink. This is the only letter in the collection with a hand-drawn illustration.

FOUR

—〰—

1864

My dear I do Cincerely Belive that we will enjoy each
others friendship again.

—David W. Walters to his wife, Rachel, April 26, 1864

AS THE WAR ENTERED ITS fourth year, the Union's coordinated strategy
focused on critical areas of the Confederacy. Union general William T. Sherman
launched the Atlanta Campaign through Georgia with the intent to capture the
manufacturing hub, and General Ulysses S. Grant led the Overland Campaign
in Virginia with the objective to destroy the Confederate Army of Northern
Virginia and capture the Confederate capital of Richmond. Both sides suffered
great loss of life during these campaigns, and war weariness plagued morale on
all fronts. The Union army faced the possibility of a manpower shortage, despite
instituting the draft in 1863. The three-year enlistments many volunteer soldiers
had signed in 1861 were due to expire.[1] In the hope of inducing men to stay in
the army, the government offered to allow regiments to keep their identities if
they retained three-quarters of their veterans. Incentives for individuals, such
as furloughs, federal and state bounties, and a chevron for uniforms convinced
about 136,000 men to reenlist.[2]

Both Isaac and John Wesley Walters reenlisted in 1864, contrary to the
inclinations they expressed in letters from late 1863.[3] Their sister-in-law Rachel Walters's letter of April 6, 1864, emphasized to her husband, David, that
she hoped he would hold to his intention not to reenlist. The pressures of
military service permeated all aspects of life. Even seemingly simple questions about the handling of an overcoat that David sent home gave rise to an
emotional discourse about the men who volunteered, the men who stayed

Despite the orderliness of this 1889 color lithograph, the Battle of Resaca pitted nearly 159,000 in combat from May 13 to May 15, 1864, resulting in combined casualties of over 5,500. The Fifth Indiana Cavalry suffered the death, injury, and capture of several of its troops, including David W. Walters. (*Library of Congress, LC-USZC4-1751*)

home, and the perceptions of how soldiers' wives should conduct themselves. The subject of the overcoat dominated the epistolary conversation between Rachel and David in the month of April; it served as a proxy by which they exposed their fears about money; health; and the ties that bound the couple, their families, and the community.[4]

Supporting a family separated by the call to military duty weighed heavily on both spouses. Rachel shouldered many duties she may not have during peacetime. Notably, Rachel began in 1864 to describe her job teaching school—education was one area of employment that had expanded for women when men left teaching posts for military service.[5] She frequently commented on student attendance, and though she did not discuss her earnings, these may have been tied to head count. Weather and road conditions factored into how many students made it to the school, as did the need of the children's families for their agricultural labor. A need to find sources of income, experienced by many women who became caretakers of farms or businesses, may have led Rachel to take the job as a teacher. Mulling over mixed feelings about teaching school in her message of Thursday, April 14, 1864, she wrote, "I would like it very well if it was not for staying away from Willie. I have not seen him since Sunday and the time seems long but I think that I will see him tomorrow evening if nothing happens more than I know of now   I must close for it is almost school time."

The situation affected both her time with her son and her letters to her husband, David. Nevertheless, David sent encouraging words about her work, writing on April 12, 1864, "[I] do hope you will have good success with your school." Two weeks later, on April 26, his worries surfaced about being a sufficient provider for his family: "[Y]ou spoke about having wet feet   my dear have you went to teaching school with out getting you a pair of boots   if you have it grieves me verry much   if you have not got money enough to make you cufartable let me know by the return of mail and I will spare you some. . . . I send all the money I think I can spare handy but I have not sent enough." Rachel responded on May 3, 1864, reassuring David that she understood his exceptional situation: "I know that you earn it by the hardest and I think that I should not spend it foolishly."

The war created circumstances, if only temporarily, that changed the traditional roles for men and women. Rachel and David, like many spouses, had to negotiate the impact of these changes through their correspondence. From the numerous references to movements between towns and boarding situations, and time with her son, Willard, it appears Rachel juggled her many responsibilities, sometimes with the assistance of family and neighbors. With her husband she shared financial responsibilities, receiving support from him but also supplementing his means, if only, sometimes, with stamps to help them continue exchanging letters.

Class and race confronted David in profound ways during this same period. His letter of April 17, 1864, contains the only record of his discussion of slavery. After months of deployment in the border state of Kentucky, he told his wife of "the country about richmond, lexington, paris, mt sterling and here is verry nice. nice houses but no barns good stalk but little. the poor man is no better than a darky   you see them along the pike hammering stone with the slave   you see the effects of slvry."[6] His perspective focused on poor whites, framing an antislavery sentiment around the impact on the race and class with whom he identified. At this point in the war, David Walters, with over nineteen months in service, had undoubtedly wrestled with the issues that brought him and the nation into conflict. He rarely wrote of them.

On May 1, David's regiment left its camps in Kentucky and began marching south through the state and through Tennessee. The frequent and steady communication between David and Rachel in the early spring came to a notable end when the Fifth Indiana Cavalry joined the Atlanta Campaign. In northern Georgia, David's regiment took part in combat at Varnell's Station on May 7 and 9, the Demonstration on Dalton on May 9–13, and the Battle of Resaca on May 13–15. At Resaca, Georgia, on May 13, 1864, Union forces began probing defenses set up by Confederate general Joseph E. Johnston. The following day, fighting occurred across the whole line, but Union forces were unable to make a successful breach. On May 15, attacks continued until Union forces successfully crossed the Oostanaula River on the right flank, threatening the Confederate positions. Confederate forces withdrew from the defenses at Resaca, ending the fighting.[7] The Battle of Resaca was one of the first, and one of the bloodiest, battles of the Atlanta Campaign.

Despite the advance of the Union forces, the toll on the Fifth Indiana Cavalry was severe. By the account of Sergeant John S. Louderback, the regiment suffered the loss of twenty-five men as killed, wounded, or missing, including David Walters and five others from Company I who had been taken as prisoners. Louderback delivered the distressing news to his friend's wife, Rachel, on May 22. He offered brief consolation, writing, "Your Husband was a good & brave soldier & I am sorry to loose him from the Company. If you get any word from him, Pleas let me . . . here from you."

No official system existed to inform family members of the status of sick, wounded, missing, imprisoned, or killed soldiers. Comrades, like Louderback, commanding officers, chaplains, or hospital workers took on the duties to send the available information. Soldiers and officers held in prisoner-of-war (POW) camps could send and receive mail, but the mail was limited, reviewed, and slow. Both Union and Confederate authorities restricted POW letters to one sheet of paper, and censors examined all incoming and outgoing material. Mail exchange for POWs took place at designated locations under flag of truce.

The exchange of prisoners, however, had ground to a standstill the year prior to the capture of David Walters. Early in the conflict, the number of prisoners remained relatively small, and their captors found room for them in forts, camps, or prisons. However, not until 1862 did both sides agree to a formal exchange program. If one side had more prisoners than the other during exchanges, the extra prisoners were paroled, if they promised to refrain from rejoining the army until they were formally exchanged. The system broke down as the Confederacy adopted a policy in May 1863 threatening to kill or reenslave captured African American soldiers and their officers, and, following the fall of Vicksburg in July 1863, declared paroled prisoners of the Confederate army as effectively exchanged and allowed them to rejoin the military.[8] As a result, the number of prisoners held by both sides rapidly increased, and the POW camps exceeded their capacities. Camp Douglas and Elmira Prison administered by the Union and Andersonville Prison and Florence Stockade administered by the Confederacy became shocking examples of places of contemptible treatment and staggering death rates as a result of malnutrition and inadequate shelter. Despite pressure on the Union command from some members of the public, newspaper publishers, and politicians in the North and South to resume the exchanges, it held fast until a new exchange system including African American soldiers was finally agreed to in February 1865. It came too late for many prisoners who had perished under terrible conditions.[9]

The news of David's predicament was followed by more sad losses for the Walters family. In May, cousin Joseph Walters died in battle in Virginia. John Wesley Walters had returned home to Royal Center, Indiana, but he died there of disease on June 28. By way of his sister-in-law Rachel, Isaac Walters had learned of one brother's death and another brother's imprisonment. Isaac continued to write to Rachel through the summer and autumn of 1864 while he faced nearly daily skirmishes in the siege of Petersburg, Virginia, as the Union forces slowly began their takeover of the critical rail lines into the city.

As the war continued into late 1864, the country faced a critical election. The Democrats controlled the Indiana state legislature and stalled provisions for absentee voting by the soldiers, who tended to favor the Republican Party. Governor Morton and President Lincoln responded by encouraging the army to facilitate furloughs so at least a portion of Indiana's soldiers could return home to cast their ballots in the 1864 election.[10] Isaac referred to this action in his November 24, 1864, letter, saying, "Some of the boys have just returned from Ind which have been on Furlough   they look well & all bring good news. they were Furloughed to give old Abe a hoist but dident get there in time but the Old Gentleman got through Safe any how." The election of 1864 resulted in a shift back to Republican leadership in the Indiana legislature and the reelection of Morton as governor as well as the reelection of the "Old Gentleman," as Isaac called President Lincoln.

David W. Walters to Rachel J. Walters

Knoxville
January sunday the 31/ 64

This day finds me well and i do sincerly hope when these few
lines Comes to hand they may find you enjoying the same blessing
of god   we are doing infantry duty, there is nothing like being
all parts of a soldier   i can scout with any of them and Can run a
battery or Carry a knapsack but i will take the horse in preference of
all the rest   rachel let me know where isaac is i would like to write
to him   you will pray for me   i know you will teach little willy
that he has a pa in dixez fighting rebbs   we have been in about 25
engagements   i have escaped fine   how thank we ought to bee,
the weather is like the full month of aprile but we have had some verry
cool weather   tell the boys[11] to write and will answer as i have time
now   phobe i have not forgotten you in your lonely houres to pray
that we meat again   i believe i will close for the present by saying
write soon

i remain your affectionate husband
David Walters
Of Walkers Cavalry
Walkers Cavalry[12]

RACHEL J. WALTERS TO DAVID W. WALTERS

Star City Pulaski Co Ind
Wednesday February 10th /64

My Dear and much loved companion,

with a thankful heart I this morning seat myself to write you a few lines in answer to your very kind and ever welcome letters of which I received two[13] day before yesterday and read with much satisfaction they being the first letters that I had received in ten weeks and you may know that they was gladly received. I am well as usual   I was weighed while I was gone to Center   I weighed one hundred and thirty lbs   I was gone three weeks   Willie got sick while I was gone the doctor said that he was takeing the conjection of the brain but it had not got fairly settled   he is a great deal better now so much so that he can walk about the floor   he is very cross but I am willing to put up with that if he does not get any worse   I feel very thankful to the good being for his kindness in spareing his life for I was so uneasy about him   I wrote a letter to pap and he come down to Center last monday and I come with him on the train to star City but the doctor said that I must not take him home that night but Phebe has come after ~~him~~ me to day and I guess that it will not hurt him to take him out to day   Phebe sends you her best respects   Emeline said that I must tell you something about her   well I think that Em is trying to do what she thinks to be right   she has joined meeting and she will not go to a dance or any thing of the kind   she went to meeting last sunday night and got a beau   it is Mr Frances Groul   a brother of Susan's   I guess that he is a very nice young man.

but I must close as willie is crying and I must get ready to start home please write as soon as you get this for I am so uneasy when I do not hear from you often   so no more at present but remember me at a throne of grace

yours in love
Rachel Walters[14]

David W. Walters to Rachel J. Walters

64

Comberlin gap[15]

february the 14

Dear Companion,

    once more i am permitted to write you afew lines in order to let you know how i am [*illegible deletion*] getting along this plesant sabbath morning finds me well and harty and i do hope when these few lines Comes to hand They will find you well   after a long and weary march of five days we rech the gap 80 mi. we expect to go across to Camp nelson[16] before it   i have written four letters since i [*illegible deletion*] have receive an answer   i stood the march well   we averaged 16 miles a day   tell the boys to write[17]   there is 38 pieces of artillery at this place   i will close until i get better ink

David Walters[18]

RACHEL J. WALTERS AND PHEBE A. (WARD) DUNKIN
TO DAVID W. WALTERS

Star City Pulaski Co Ind
Wednesday evening April 6th /64

Dear David,

I improve the present opportunity by writing you a few lines to let
you know how we are getting along. I am well at present and hope that
these few lines may find you enjoying the same good blessing of god. I
received your ever welcome letter of March 30th[19] and was glad to hear
from you   I also received those pieces of writing   I think they
are very nice, but I have not received the pamphlet yet.

I am glad that your mind is with mine about reenlisting   I hope
that it will remain so and not do as Isaac did.[20] I have not seen Isaac
to talk with him any yet. I went to Logansport with Phebe and Arthur
and when we got back to Center I stopped and staid until last saturday
evening they expected Isaac home from Ohio every day but he did not
come til saturday evening   he got off the train when I got on and I
only just got to speak to him

I was at Mr McCauley's a little while last saturday   Mrs
McCauley has been very sick but she is better   she had the
congestive fever.[21] the rest of them are well   I saw Martha saturday
evening   she said that she had received a letter from you   she
said that she had not answered it yet but I suppose that she has before
this time. Wesley stated in his letter that he had received a letter
from you but did not say whether he had answered it or not. I did not
commence my school last monday   it was so rainy and bad that the
children could not get there but I expect to commence next monday.
I expect that you would like to slip into the school room and take
me on surprise but it would not do you any more good than it would
me   Mary Ann was well when I was there   she got a letter
from Charles a few days before   I believe that he was at Russleville
Ind   he is in the 12th cavalry   I had my miniature and Willies
taken while I was at Center. Our heifer has got a nice calf   I ~~that~~
think that she will make a better cow than old streak   uncle Henry
Walters has traded farms with John Clary and has moved up by sam
Blacks   that overcoat that you sent home is at uncle Henry's and he
wants to buy it. please let me know in your next letter whether you are

willing to sell it and what you think it is worth so that I can give him an answer. I believe I will close for the present as Phebe wants to write a little please excuse all mistakes and write as soon as you get this

> yours in love,
> Rachel

> [*Postscript continues on side margin.*]
> direct to Star City I will try and
> send more stamps next time

[*Correspondence by Phebe A. (Ward) Dunkin continues on the same sheet.*]

> Star city
> April the 6th 1864

My Dear brother

After a shamefull silence which I beg you to pardon I again attempt to converse with you through the silent language of the pen   This leaves me in good health of boddy more so than you ever saw me   if my mind was composed I should enjoy myself well but alass that can never be in this low ground of sorrow   Only 4 weeks and a long year has flown since I received the last embrace and kissed those lips that never gave me nought but joy   O David you can never appreciate the value of a companion untill you loose one   But a few few more days and I shall joyn him in the glorious land   David pray for me that I may prove faithfull untill death   My Desire is that you may grow in grace and in the knowledge of the truth   David I have got a verry [*illegible deletion*] nice grave stone for my Dear husband   it has hands as representing our meeting and two flags and a verse which reads as follows:

> Dear Isaac though flowers may bloom to deay
> And loved ones alike them may soon pass away
> Yet there is one flower that neer will depart
> And thats thy loved immage enstamped on my heart
> Nay thy immage from me shall never be riven
> But prove as a compass to guide me to heaven

David I expect you think I do not want to write to you   if you do
you think wrong   I have not had the opportunity   please excuse
me and write when convenient

Your well wishing sister
Phebe

To her brother David[22]

DAVID W. WALTERS TO RACHEL J. WALTERS

Camp near Paris
April 12 /64

[*illegible deletion*] Dear Companion,

Once more i am permited to answer yours which i received a few minutes ago   your kind letter found me well and i do hope these few lines will find you enjoying the same good blessing i see by the papers that our army and Comberland army[23] are ordered [*illegible deletion*] to nashvile so when you write direct [*illegible deletion*] to the army of the ohio   i supose we will soon bee in active servis and it will be impossible for me to write verry often so you must put up with a few letters but i will do the best i can   i do hope you will have good success with your school   you spoke about that Coat[24]   There is something very strange about that Coat   i sent me overcoat with sergt hohn S loudesbacks[25] Clothing to his residence in fulton, fulton Co and if this is the [*illegible deletion*] overcoat they had no buisness with it   if i get holt some of them ill ring there necks   i never sent but one Coat home   i would have told you to go and get it but sergeant said it was safe there   i never sent dady a overcoat   i suppose They have worn it partly out by this time so you can sell it for what you can get   it ought to bee [*illegible deletion*] worth 10 dollars but sell it for what you Can   if i had hold of uncle id make him think of a soldier o poor Phebe & how i pity poor her in her lonly hours[26]   may god Bless poor phebe   i think of her & yes verry often hard & verry hard it must bee to loose a Companion   o god forbid that this should befall us & poor phebe   o how i would like to see her   i believe i will Close for the presant   write soon

yours as ever
David W. Walters

5th Cavalry regt
Ind vol
Co I
Army of the
Ohio[27]

Writing to her husband, David, on April 12, 1864, Rachel J. Walters
discussed news that she had received from his brother John Wesley while
John Wesley's regiment was in Louisiana in March. John Wesley's letter
is not in the collection; however, this envelope that likely carried it is.
(*National Postal Museum, Smithsonian Institution, 1991.0291.154*)

RACHEL J. WALTERS TO DAVID W. WALTERS

Star City Pulaski Co Indiana
Tuesday April 12th 1864

Dear David

 I again seat myself in order to try to write you a few lines to let you
know that I am well at present, and I do hope that those few lines may
find you enjoying the same good blessing of God

 I received your very kind letter of April 2nd[28] last saturday evening
and read it with much interest. I also received the ring that was in the
letter I think that it is a very nice ring it is so small that I have
to wear it on my little finger it is too small for any of the rest. I
shall keep it as a token of love and respect that you have for me my
dear you have mine in return. I received them things that you left with

Wm. House for me   it was two thimbles a belt a string of buttons
and that ring of yours   I received them last sunday morning. I am
going to send you a couple of Pictures and want to know ~~them or not~~
whether you know them or not. I am now at the school house and it
is noon time. my school is not very full the roads are so bad and there
is so much water on the ground the children cannot get here   I
did not commence until yesterday   it was so rainy and bad that I
thought that I had better wait a few days. I did not get to see Isac to
talk with him any   I got on the cars at Royal Center when he got
off and I only had time to speak to him. I am sorry that I could not visit
with him a while, David I do not want you to think that I did not want
to send you ~~you~~ that money and stamps that you wrote for such is not
the case   I am not only willing but anxious that you should have
any thing that I have got that would make you comfortable   the
reason that I did not send more was because I was afraid that you
would not get it and I thought that it would be better to send a part at
a time   There is to be a prayer meeting here to morrow night   I
wish that you could attend but as you cannot attend prayer meeting
here I hope that you can there

I must close for it is time to take up school   please excuse all
mistakes and my poor writing for I am in a hurry so no more at present

yours in love
Rachel J. Walters

[*Letter continues on a later date.*]

Thursday April 14th 64

Dear David

I am now seated in order to answer your letters of which I received
two last night and read them with much interest   They found me
well and at prayer meeting. we had a very good meeting. It has been so
rany that I could not take this letter to the office and as I had not much
to write I thought that I would answer them that I got last night on the
same paper. You will please excuse me for so doing and I will try and do
better next time. I also received a letter from Wesley last night[29]   he
was well and at Alexandria Louisiana but they expected to move right
on to Schreers port[30] distance about 175 miles

I am trying to teach school but the roads are so muddy and it rains so much that there is not many of the scholars that can get here but I am in hopes that it will be better next week   I think that I would like it very well if it was not for staying away from Willie. I have not seen him since Sunday and the time seems long but I think that I will see him tomorrow evening if nothing happens more than I know of now   I must close for it is almost school time   please excuse my short letter for the present I will close please write soon   Remember me when this you see   Though many miles apart we be   Remember that those lines were pened by one who is your constant friend

yours in love
Rachel J. Walters[31]

David W. Walters to Rachel J. Walters

Winchester Ky Apr the 17/ 64
& Camp of the 5th Ind Scouts
Camp near Winchester

Dear Companion

i once more resume my seat in order to let you know how i am a getting along   this pleasant sabath morning finds me well hopeing these few lines may find you enjoying the same blessing   we left camp on the 14th   we are ordered to stay here untill further orders   i suppose there is letters in Camp for me but i Cant get them untill we return to the Command   my Dear i want you to [*illegible deletion*] heare from me as often as possible   this why i write while on the scout this late letter i received on the 12th   There is about 250 of us here   i think weare we are stationed in squads to force the draft properly[32]   i think the Comd is at nickelsville Ky[33]   the country about richmond, lexington, paris, mt sterling and here is verry nice. nice houses but no barns good stalk but little. the poor man is no better than a darky   you see them along the pike hammering stone with the slave   you see the effects of slvry   I Belive i will Close for the presant

yours in love
D.W.W.

Direct to the
Army of
the Ohio
and to the regt[34]

Rachel J. Walters to David W. Walters

Star City, Pulaski Co Ind
Monday noon April 18th 1864

Dear companion,

I now seat myself to answer your ever welcome letters of April 10th and 12th[35] which came to hand day before yesterday   They found me well except a head ache   I had a light chill yesterday   I think it was caused from getting my feet wet, but I feel tolorable well to day and I think that I will get along without haveing any more. I also received the miniature taken on the horse[36]   I think it looks very nice but I have not received that tract that you spoke of that is a very nice song composed by Rudolph. I have had very good luck with my school so far only it has not been as full as I would have liked   I have thirteen scholars to day   I think when the roads settle that there will be several more. About that over coat[37] I will try to explain to you what I have heard about it, it ~~was it~~ is the coat that was sent to Mr. Louderbacks and it was brought from there by a preacher and left at uncle Henry's for dady and he paid the freight on it which he said was 50 cts and he sent me word that he did not need the coat and I might have it and when I seen him he told me the same and I intended on going there after it when I was at Center in the winter but Willie got sick and I could not go, and when I was down the last time they had moved up by Mr. Blacks and taken it with them and I saw William in Center and I asked him about it and he said that it was there and his father wanted to buy it if I ~~will~~ would sell it and I told him that I did not know but I would see about it. So I thought that I would write and ask you about it as I did not know what it was worth nor whether you would like for me to sell it or not   I have got me a new cloak and hat at last. the cloak cost six dollars and seventy five cents and hat cost 2.80 cts   I would not mind wearing them if you was here to see me wear them but as it is I do not feel right for the soldiers wives here have the name of spending all that their husbands send them for finery and I am determined that I will not do that, the clothes that I had Willies likeness taken[38] in cost two dollars   his pants are black cloth and his waist blue velvet they are trimmed in small brass buttons. Chris

Bingaman is married again   he married Rebecca Ristter   I
think that his wife has not been dead over three months. As I have
nothing very interesting to write I will close by asking you to write
soon and remembering me at a throne of grace so no more at present

> yours in bonds of love
> Rachel J. Walters
>
> N.B. I have forgotten whether I told you that
> Eli's had lost another babe   it was a
> littl e girl it lived to be four days old.[39]

DAVID W. WALTERS TO RACHEL J. WALTERS

Nicholsville, Ky
Apr the 26th /64

Dear Rachel

Tis with much pleasure that I improve the presant by writeing these few lines this day find me well   hopeing you are the same   we returned to the command yesterday   The minaters had been here a couple of days but as we had orders to return to the Command our mail was not sent to us   I think the picturs are verry nice[40]   I would not know Willy but yours [*illegible deletion*] is very hansome. if you had been standing and your hat on it would have suited me better but it is nice enough   you spoke about having wet feet   my dear have you went to teaching school with out getting you a pair of boots   if you have it grieves me verry much   if you have not got money enough to make you cufartable let me know by the return of mail and I will spare you some. My dear I thought you was old enough to not mind what p people says. I want you to buy any thing that make you and Willy happy. my dear I have not sent money enough to buy yours and Willies Clothes since I have been in the army   I send all the money I think I can spare handy but I h have not sent enough

N B[41] if I had a holt of some of them they would wish they never saw a soldier   id slap the verry pis out of some of them   id let them know how the poor soldier gets his money the Courdly pupps stay at home and pester the ones that are fiting   now rachel I want you to Clothe your self well and not listen to every shit ass   if you have not got a pair of B Boots go and get them imeditaely   if you have not got the [*illegible deletion*] money get them on time [*illegible deletion*]

I earn this money I send you By hard and Brave soldiering and tis none of their Business. I dont send you money to lay up but for to make you Comfortable

NB now rachel I know by your likeness that you are not well or are fretting your self very much. my dear what did Christ say to his disciples in regard to [*illegible deletion*] healing he said ye of little faith   my dear I do Cincerely Belive that we will enjoy each others friendship again. I will close

Yours as ever
D. W.

Directions David W. Walters
Co I   5th Ind Cav
Army of the
Ohio[42]

Rachel J. Walters to David W. Walters

Star City Pulaski Co Ind
May 3d/ 1864

My Dear David,

I improve the present by writing you a few lines to let you know that
I am well and I sincerely hope that these lines will find you enjoying
good health for which I feel thankful to the god of heaven that he has
blessed you with such good health and my earnest prayer is that he may
still bless you with the same. my dear I am sorry that you have to go
so far away again, but will trust you to gods care praying that he may
shield you from evil or harm and O may he hasten the time that you
may return home. I walked to Star city last night after school and was
well paid for my trip for I received two letters[43] and two small books
or tracts from you. I have read them all and think that they are very
nice my dear if it was not for the good and kind letters that I receive
from you it seems to me that I never could stand it. I am glad that you
have received the miniatures for I was afraid that you never would
get them. About them boots my dear I think that they would be so
warm for summer that I could not wear them and I have got my shoes
fixed as they only leaked around the sole where the pegs had drawed
out   the mud and water have dried up now so that I can get about
very well. my dear I think that I have clothes enough to make me
comfortable, but I do not want to spend my money foolishly. I know
that you earn it by the hardest and I think that ~~had~~ I should not spend
it foolishly

I am ~~try~~ still trying to teach school   I have had very good
luck so far and the prospect begins to look better   I have twenty
two scholars to day and I have 26 names on the roll. six new scholars
to day and there is some more to come yet. I saw doctor Osborn
yesterday evening when I was at star city but I did not have time
to go to the house but he said that they was as well as usual. King
Dick died last friday morning   he was only sick two days he
had just been to the army as teamster   he had only been home
two weeks   Josephine Dick is sick now but she was better this
morning   old Mr Vicars is dead   he was as well as common last
sunday and he fell off his chair dead   please tell me in your next
letter whether you know a young man in your company by the name

of Corbit and whether you know what become of him ~~Mrs McCau~~
Mrs McCauley told me that his folks had not heard from him for
some time   they thought that he had been taken prisoner but they
had not heard from him for so long that they did not know what had
become of him and I told her that I would write and ask you. There
is a call here for twenty thousand more men from thi s state for one
hundred days   I believe that ~~they are to have~~ they are to have the
monthly wages but no bounty   I saw grand mother Reys the other
day   she sends you her best respects and christian love. as my paper
is abot filled and it is all that I have with me I will have to close hopeing
to hear from you soon and often

                                        I close yours in bonds of love
                                        Rachel[44]

Rachel J. Walters to David W. Walters

Star City Pulaski Co Ind,
Saturday May 14th/ 64

My Dear and much loved companion,

I again seat myself in order to answer your very kind and ever welcome letter of May 9th[45] which came to hand yesterday evening and was gladly received and read with much satisfaction. It found me well and I hope that this may find you enjoying the same blessing of health. I am still trying to teach school   the prospect begins to look a little fairer   my school averaged from twenty four to twenty eight this week   this looks a little more encouraging. This is Saturday and I have been covering corn for pap this forenoon and I expect to help this afternoon. he has got about 18 acres planted and I dont know how much more he is going to plant. Willie is well   he is very well pleased to see me come home   he always runs to meet me he says that he is ma's boy and pa's boy to   he says that his pa is down in dixie fighting rebels and I asked him what he thought that pa would fetch him when he came home and he said he thought that pa would fetch him some little boots. but they are ready to go out to the field now and I must go to and then I can finish after while.

[Letter continues on the next day.]

May 15th

Dear David,

as I was too tired to write any more last evening, I now proceed to ~~answer~~ finish   this good sabbath day finds me as well as usual   I walked down to sabbath school this morning as I have a class   I thought that I must attend and after sabbath school I ~~that~~ thought that I would walk down to star city, so I am now at Martha's   she is well as usual   she received a letter from Isaac last evening   he is in the hospital a Washington   he has been very sick with the lung fever[46] but is getting better so that he could walk about the room [*illegible deletion*]   I received a letter from Emeline this morning   she was well but not very well satisfied   she does not like her step mother very well. I think that picture you sent to Martha for me is the nicest one that you have ever had taken yet   it looks so manly and good. I got me a new pair of shoes last night   they are very high and good for walking   they cost me two dollars an sixty cents. I dont think that I will have wet feet now. The war news are more favorable than ever now. they all think that war cannot last much longer for my part I certainly hop that it will not there has been two hard battles in Virginia lately[47]

I believe that I will close for the present by asking you to remember me at a throne of grace for I feel that I need the prayers of all gods people

I will close hopeing to hear from you as often as possible and I will try to write oftener that I have been doing. I will send you a few stamps in this letter I would send you more at a time but I am afraid that you might not get them there is many such accidents hapens so no more at present but I still remain your true and affectionate companion until death

Rachel J. Walters to her very dear companion
David W. Walters[48]

On May 22, 1864, First Sergeant John S. Louderback wrote to inform Rachel J. Walters that her husband, David, had been captured at the Battle of Resaca. (*National Postal Museum, Smithsonian Institution, 1991.0291.108*)

JOHN S. LOUDERBACK TO RACHEL J. WALTERS

May 22d 1864
Camp near Carters Station Georgia[49]

Mrs D W Walters

    I am vairy Sorry to inform you that your Husband D W Walters was Was taken prisioner on the 15th ins at Recaca Georgia[50] to gether with five other from Co. I   They loss in our Regt at this place in Killed Wounded & missing was 25   our Regt took that day of Prisioners 150 Burned a part of they Reb trane & took 50 Horses and mewls   Turned their artillery on then but being pressed had to leave it   This was a vairy hard fight lasting three days   What our en tire loss was I Cannot Say   they Reble loss in killed & wounded was be twirst 7 &10 thousand   took 12 Piece of artillery   We had a complete victory   We ar now 12 miles be lo Kingston[51]   They will make another stand here & we expect to have an other heavy enggagement at this place

Your Husband was a good & brave soldier & I am sorry to loose him from the Company

If you get any word from him[52] Pleas let me [illegible deletion] here from you

We also had one man killed & one wounded in the Company

My respects to all enquiring friends

Yours with respect
John S. Louderback
1st Sergt Condy Co. "I"[53]

RACHEL J. WALTERS TO DAVID W. WALTERS

Star-City Pulaski Co Ind
Monday May 23d/ 64
At the school house

My Dear and much beloved companion

after a silence of one week I again resume my seat in order to pen
you a few lines to let you know that I am yet on the land and among
the living and have not forgotten you   no dearest never can I forget
you nor the many pleasant hours I have spent with you. those were the
happiest day of my life should I ever see such times again I should know
how to enjoy them. It is now over a week since I have received a letter[54]
but I hope that it will not be that much longer. seventeen months
have now passed since I last saw that form which for the last five years
has been the object of my earthly affections but my sincere prayer is
that your life may be spared and that we may soon have the privilege
of seeing each other face to face and singing the songs of zion and
mingling our friendly voices together in praiseing God. this has always
been my desire and I do hope that I may yet have this privilege. There
has been some very hard fighting done lately[55]

I heard yesterday that cousin Joseph Walters that was with Isaac
in the 20th was killed how I pity his poor mother if it is so   I dont
think that Isaac was in the fight, but to change the subject my school
is not very full today as the most of the people are planting corn and
have to keep their children at home as hands are so scarce. pap is done
planting he planted between 35 and 40 acres I believe. Willie is well
he can sing so many little songs I do wish that you could hear him it
sounds so cunning for such a little boy   he has a little union song
that he sings sometimes

It is this; I'll take my knapsack on my back, My musket on my shoulder
And away I'll go to the war with pa
And be a gallant soldier.

I was at sabbath school yesterday in the forenoon and to meeting
in the after noon   the Sabbath school was here and the meeting at
Olive 'branch   Mr. Caler preached. I wish if you can that you would
tell me in your next letter how many stamps you have received since

you sent me that dollar   the reason that I asked this I wanted to
know whether you have got all that I have sent you or not.

I believe that I will close for the present as I have nothing very
interesting to write please excuse all mistakes for I am in a hurry.

hopeing to hear from you soon

> I close yours in true love
> Rachel
>
> to her companion[56]

RACHEL J. WALTERS TO DAVID W. WALTERS

Star City Indiaia
Thursday June 2d 1863[57]

My Dear companion

    after a long silence I once more attempt to write you a few lines to let you know that I have not forgotten you. no I dont believe that there is a moment in the day that I am not thinking of you. It is now three weeks since I have heard from you. I have written three letters since I have received one but I will try to look on the bright side of the picture. This morning finds me well and still trying to teach school. I am now at Allen Miller's. I have been boarding at Milton Venard's this week. I do not know where I will board next week. I have been teaching almost eight weeks and there is five weeks more of school I was at Fulton last saturday on a visit to uncle Joseph Seller's they were well. Milton Sellers was married last thrusday to Miss Susan Martin a lady living in Fulton. Samuel Sellers told me that Mrs Louderback had received a letter from her husband a few days before he also said that the regiment was in Alabama. I have not heard from Isaac and Wesley for some time. the paper's state that James Torrence was killed in the battle and cousin Joseph Walters was mortally wounded.[58] Willie is well he has a new song to sing for me every time I go home. next sunday is our meeting day I wish that I could see you at meeting once more but I hope that you have good meetings there and can enjoy you self at them. I hope these lines will find you as well as they leave me pray for me dear David that I may live more in the discharge of my duty that I may trust you to his kind care and protection while in the enemies land and that he may grant you a safe and speedy return

    wheat looks well the weather here is very fine, but I must close as Mrs. Miller is about ready to start to the office. please write as soon as you can so no more at present

yours in bonds of love
Rachel J. Walters

To
David Walters[59]

ISAAC WALTERS TO RACHEL J. WALTERS

Camp in the Field June 8th /64[60]

Dear Sister

After this long delay I compose myself in order to drop a few
lines to you once more in order that you may know that I have not
forgotten you. I Should have wrote to you long ago but I have So many
to write to I can hardly get around. there are a good many I promised
to write to that I have not penned a line to yet & I fear I never will to
Some of them. you must not think hard of me for not writing Sooner
or coming to pay you a visit Either fo I dident get to more than half
the places around there I Intended to go to.[61] no Doubt but you felt
disappointed because I dident get out there but I doubt whether you
felt much more Disappointed than I did myself for I fully intended
to go & had Set a day to go but it rained all day that day & after that
it was to late my time was So near out I had to get ready to Start to
Indianapolis. I Spent to much of my time in Ohio to have a good Visit
in Indiana but it Seemed Impossible for me to get away any Sooner.
we have plenty of Music here if you would call the Firing of Guns
music   both Day and night lately there is more Fighting done
in the night than in the day time   the Rebels have charged our
works Several times lately in the night but have been nicely repulsed
every time   they are becoming very much Discouraged & Say
they want the war to Close on any terms   they think if they lose
Richmond the war will close right away   So the Prisoners Say. all
the boys that are left are well & in good Spirits   they feel Confident
of Success. joseph walters is Dead he died on the 19th of last month
at Fredricksburg[62]   James Torrence was killed also   This is
all you was acquaited with   Jerry Pherson is wounded & sent
away. my health is reasonably good & I trust this may find you well &
happy   Write Soon

Yours Truly
Isaac Walters

[*Postscript continues on side margin.*]
Excuse this Envelop for it is all I have[63]

ISAAC WALTERS TO RACHEL J. WALTERS

Camp of the 20th Ind Vols[64]
July 14th /64

Dear Sister

After this long delay I Seat myself in order to Answer your most kind & welcome letter which came to hand about a week ago but I have not had time to Answer it until the present time as we moved the next day & have not been Settled long enough till to day to Send away any Mail. I hope you will not think hard of me as you will See I am writing at the Earliest moment possible.

Your letter was long looked for & most thankfully received although it brought Sad news to me. I never can forget that Dear Brother of mine[65]   how Dear are the Memories of the past & if I could only have Seen him & conversed with him it would not Seem So hard to give him up. I feel as though I had lost my dearest & best friend one that was always true to me & one in whom I could rely   I feel as though this Earth never could restore what the Lord has taken away. but I hope my Dear Departed Brother is happy in the paradise prepared for the Saints in the Kingdom above where all is joy & happiness for Ever   I hope we may all be So unspeakably happy as to meet him in that happy home when we are done with the things of this Sinful & unfriendly world your letter found me enjoying reasonable good health although not as well as I have been in my life time   I was very glad to hear that you was well & also that of your little boy   I hope this good blessing may Still attend you. I am very Sorry to hear that David is a Prisoner[66]   I hope he may be Speedily exchanged & have good health while he remains a prisoner   O how I would love to See him   it Seems like a long time Since we ware Separated & hope the day is not far distant when we can be permitted to enjoy each others company. Once more. Rachel I was very Sorry to know that we could not visit each other   I had fully intended to go out to your Fathers & had Set the day to go but it began to rain quite Early in the morning & rained all day   it rained So hard I could not have gone more than one mile without geting wet through   I was very Sorry as I had fully intended to pay you a visit & I know we would have had a good visit   I would liked to have had Seen Some of the Girls out there also but I hope we will be permitted to See each other Some day not far

in the future   There is fighting going on here Every day   Capt
Belle of Co B of our Regt was wounded by the fragment of Shell &
died the Same night at Eleven Oclock   no casualties in the regt
Since   we have lost Something over two hundred killed wounded
& missing in this Campaign out of the regt   the old organizations
time will be out in Eight days from this time   The boys beging
to feel almost like if they ware free men once more   I received a
piece of the trimming [*illegible deletion*] of wesleys Coffin & a lock of
his hair which looks very natural   I thank you very kindly for the
Same   I hope that peace & plenty may attend you. The weather Still
continues very hot & dry   it is almost Impossible for the troops to
march only in the night & then it is a very hard task   I have long
looked for rain but have looked in vain   I fear we are not going to
get much rain very Soon. we can Still get water by digging but there is
no water to be found on the Surface   this is the dryest time I have
Seen Since I left Kansas. The Rebels have got up into Maryland again
& are doing a good deal of Damage So the Papers State but Grant is
taking things very cool[67]   he dont Appear to let it bother him very
much   he Says he can take care of them & Richmond to at the Same
time   I hope he may   the papers Report the Rebels within Five
miles of Washington but I guess they wont get to See Old Abraham[68]
yet for a while. we are Still making Steady Advances upon Petersburg
& I think Grant will take the place After while but it is very Strongly
Fortified & will take a regular Siege   I have not had a letter from
Ohio for Some time neither from Father or Mrs Weeks   I would
like to hear how they are geting along. I believe I have nothing more of
Importance to write at present So I will close hoping this may find you
well & happy as you can be under Existing circumstances   Give my
love to Martha when you See her & Reserve a goodly portion for your
Self   I will write no more

> Yours with much Love & respect until Death.
> Isaac Walters
>
> Mrs Rachel J Walters
>
> Adieu for a while.
> Excuse my Short Letter[69]

ISAAC WALTERS TO RACHEL J. WALTERS

August 17th /64
Camp of the 20th Ind Vols[70]

Mrs Walters
Dear Sister

I once more take the opportunity of answering your very kind &
welcom letter of the 8th which chame to hand yesterday & found me
well. & in very good Spirits. I am very glad to hear of your good health
& hope this kind blessing may Still attend you. I feel very Sorry for you
that you cant hear from David   you must be on great Suspense &
you must feel very lonely but you must look upon the bright Side of the
picture & hope for the best. I think he will turn up all right Sometime if
the graybacks[71] dont Starve him to Death & I hope they will fail in this
if they undertake it   I think David has a pretty good Consitution
& will get through all right if he is only alive. well rachel we are Still
belting away at Petersburg[72]   Our Corps is now on the ~~Sou~~ North
Side of the James[73] within 12 miles of Richmond yesterday on this
Side of the River we Captured 4,oo prisoners &killed 3 Generals
one Major & two Brigadiers.[74] & it is reported that Burnsides Corps
Captured 4,000 Prisoners & 36 pieces of Artillery & Carried one
line of the Enemies works. if this be true we are Still making a little
Advancement in the good work. I wish we could kill all their Generals
then I think the war would close. we are on the Skirmish line to day
popping away at the jonnys[75] I am on reserve post writing Some times
the Shell come in rather close proximity but I am where the Minnies[76]
cant reach me yesterday Our regt was Sent out on a Reconnoisance to
feel the Strength of the enemy & had quite a Severe Skirmish with the
Graybacks but had but one man wounded. the Gospel Car is moving
Steadily along   I think the war will close Sometime or never   if
it never closes I guess there is no danger of us poor Soldiers gettin out
of a job. I will close for the present hoping soon to hear from you

Isaac Walters
Yours truly   excuse my short letter[77]

ISAAC WALTERS TO RACHEL J. WALTERS

Camp of the 20th Ind Vols[78]
Nov. 4th /64

~~Miss~~ Mrs Walters
Dear Sister,

I am now Seated in order to Answer your favor of the 23d of last
Month which is received. your letter found me well but at the present
time my health is not as good as when your letter came to hand. I have
taken cold   have quite a Severe Cough. yet I have not been to the
Doctor & am on Duty yet. I never go near the Doctor until I am obliged
to   I am very much opposed to taking medacine any where & all
the more So here in the Army. I was truly glad to learn that you enjoy
good health & also your little boy. I most Sincerely hope this kind
blessing may Still be extended toward you   I am very Sorry to hear
that you can get no tidings from David but Still I hope he is Alive &
well & will have a Speedy return home if he is a prisoner   I fear he
has a hard time of it the Rebels treat their prisoners very cruel from
all accounts but I know David has a great faculty of geting in with
Strangers & will get along if any body can. I have confidence to believe
he will get through & return home Safe after while. no Doubt but
the time Seems very long to you. but you must bear it with Christian
Fortitude alway puting your trust in him who is able to bring us out
Safe through all dangers & privations that may befall us. the more we
Sacrifice upon the Altar of our Country the the Sweeter peace will
Seem to us when it is restored & the better we will realize what peace
is. this war will be remembered as long as the world exists & very
painfully to by a great many. there are but few now but what mourns
the loss of Some kind friend dear to them. & howe many more may
be led to mourn yet there is no telling   I hope this war will soon
cease & I think it will for the rebels are Deserting by scores   they
are all geting tired of Fighting from the greatest to the smallest. we
have had another fight Since I last wrote to you. We gained nothing
this time   the fight was pretty Severe but our loss is proportionably
Small   we had but three men killed in our regiment & five or Six
wounded. One Capt among the number   All the Ind Soldiers
that were at the hospital Sick Started home this Morning on 15 days
Furlough. they will all get to vote for President[79]   I Suppose I wish

it was my lot   I think I could make good use of the time allotted me.
I think I Shall try to get a Furlough this winter & come home. if I do
will try to pay you a visit   I would like to See old Mill Creek once
more   the weather is growing quite cool & we will Soon have to go
into winter quarters   picketing is rather uncumfortable business
nowadays here we fire at each other all the time day & night   the
weather is So cold we have to have fire in our pits all the time. We are
under the enemies fire constantly. I will close by wishing you well long
life & happiness   write soon & excuse all mistakes

Yours in truth
Isaac Walters[80]

Isaac Walters to Rachel J. Walters

Camp of the 20th Ind Vols[81]
Nov. 24th/ 64

Rachel
Dear Sister

This morning I have the Opportunity of writing to you once
more   I received your favor of the 13th about three days ago but
have been So busy I could not Answer until this morning but I hope
you will pardon me me for this is the first opportunity I have had of
replying   I am glad to hear of your good health from time to time
& it may Still be your lot. I am also glad to hear that Willy is well. I
wish I could See him. does he ever Say anything about his Father   I
heared the Draft had gone off in Old Boone[82]   I also heared Some
of their names that are drafted   Some of the worst Copperheads[83]
in the Township. I hope everyone of them will have to go the next call.
I expect there is plenty of them will Desert the first chance they get.
but I say let them fight on one Side or the other. they cant do as much
harm in the rebel ranks as they can at home through the Copperhead
press. & what is more we will have a chance to put them out of the
way. Some of the boys have just returned from Ind which have been
on Furlough   they look well & all bring good news. they were
Furloughed to give old Abe a hoist but dident get there in time but the
Old Gentleman got through Safe any how. I Supose the Copperheads
in the north are mighty wrathey about it but I guess they will get over it
after a while but I think it wont be much loss if they dont. the weather
is growing quite cold again but we have had no Snow yet. we are not in
winter quarters yet & perhaps we wont be for Some time   I have
nothing of Importance to Communicate at present So I will close
hoping Soon to See you. write Soon as Convenient.

Yours Truly
Isaac Walters

R.J Walters[84]

Isaac Walters to Rachel J. Walters

Camp of the 20th Ind
Vols[85]
Dec 19th /64

Dear Sister

   After this long delay I Seat myself in order to Answer your kind
& Interesting letter which came to hand Some time ago & found me
well but I have been So busy building winter quarters & Marching
that I have not had time even to wash my own clothes let alone write.
So you must excuse me this time for it is not through neglect by any
means. I was very glad to hear from you once more to hear that you
was well I was overjoyed to hear from David[86]   feel thankful that
his life has been Spared So far & hope he may have a Speedey return
home to his Anxious Companion & Friends   I hope I may be
So happy as to as to meet him once more on Earth & while we yet
are Soldiers. I would be very happy to See him in deed. well I must
tell you Something about our March. the 5th Corps & Our Division
was Sent on a raid all under Command of Gen Warren.[87] we made
a raid on the Weldon Railroad tore it up & burned it for about 20
miles   Destroyed ane 1,000 bushels of corn that had been bought
& Stored for the Rebel government   made a march of over 80 miles
& returned in Six days   we met with no loss except a few men that
were Murdered   we for retaliation of this horrible deed burned
every house within one mile on each Side of the road for over 20 miles.
we have now began to build winter quarters. we have Received Joyful
news from Gen Sherman[88]   the paper reports that he has taken
Savannah with Eleven thousand prisoners[89]   this is joyful news &
I think the war is drawing very near its close. for my part I doubt very
much that we will have another Summers Campaign. I think every
thing looks very fovorable on our Side & very gloomy on the Side of the
rebels   I will close for the present

Yours truly   Write Again
Isaac Walters

excuse all Mistakes for I See they are plenty[90]

NOTES

1. In contrast, the Confederate government at the start of the war had authorized the formation of an army consisting of one hundred thousand men for twelve months, but after recruitment slowed and manpower shortages grew, the government set stricter enlistment terms and forced retention (McPherson, *Battle Cry of Freedom*, 318).

2. McPherson, *Battle Cry of Freedom*, 719–720.

3. Isaac Walters reenlisted at Camp Bullock, Virginia, on February 15, 1864 (US National Homes for Disabled Volunteer Soldiers, 1866–1938, Isaac Walters, Pvt., Co. F, 20 Ind. Inf.; Civil War, RG 15; NA-Washington). John Wesley Walters reenlisted in Algiers, Louisiana, on January 2, 1864, and was due a $400 bounty (compiled military service record, John Wesley Walters, Pvt., Co. I, 46 Ind. Inf.; Civil War, RG 94; NA-Washington).

4. The subject of the overcoat featured in letters of April 6, 12, and 18 and influenced David Walters's letter of April 26. Only a few days lapsed between the exchanges. The couple accounted for other letters sent and received in the spring that are not in the collection. Six envelopes (1991.0291.149, 1991.0291.157, 1991.0291.168, 1991.0291.169, 1991.0291.171, and 1991.0291.172) from this period do not have matching letters, but they show that David wrote often while deployed in Kentucky. His envelope with the latest date was postmarked in Nicholasville, Kentucky, on April 30, 1864 (1991.0291.171), and his latest dated letter (1991.0291.39), also from Nicholasville, was written on April 26, 1864, with matching envelope (1991.0291.40) postmarked on April 27, 1864.

5. Perlmann and Margo, *Women's Work?: American Schoolteachers*, 87.

6. The Emancipation Proclamation did not free enslaved people in states loyal to the Union, including Kentucky and the other border states.

7. McPherson, *Battle Cry of Freedom*, 744–745.

8. McPherson, *Battle Cry of Freedom*, 792.

9. McPherson, *Battle Cry of Freedom*, 791–793.

10. Benton, *Voting in the Field*, 281–292.

11. *The boys* likely refers to David Walters's brothers, Isaac and John Wesley, who frequently corresponded with both David and his wife, Rachel.

12. The envelope (1991.0291.33) for this letter (1991.0291.32) is postmarked "KN[OXVILLE] / TEN / FEB 8 / 64" over a three-cent George Washington stamp placed in the upper left corner. It was addressed "Mrs D. W. Walters / Starcity / Pulaski Co. / Ind." A pencil notation, "too dim," was added, likely by a family member, after the letter was received and before it was donated to the museum. The letter was written on stationery embossed with a paper manufacturer's mark.

13. There is only one letter (1991.0291.32), which is dated January 31, 1864, from David Walters in the collection between this and Rachel Walters's letter of December 22–23, 1863 (1991.0291.53).

14. The letter (1991.0291.54) was written on blue-lined stationery embossed with a crown over a shield. A matching envelope has not been identified.

15. The Cumberland Gap sits at the borders of Kentucky, Tennessee, and Virginia.

16. Camp Nelson, Kentucky, was a Union supply depot and a training center for African American soldiers.

17. *The boys* likely refers to David Walters's brothers, Isaac and John Wesley, who frequently corresponded with both David and his wife, Rachel.

18. The quality of the iron gall ink noted by David Walters is evident in the uneven shading within words. The letter (1991.0291.34) was written on blue-lined stationery embossed "Nayasset Co" set in a shield. A matching envelope has not been identified.

19. The referenced letter, dated March 30, is not in the collection.

20. Isaac Walters reenlisted in the Twentieth Indiana Infantry when the regiment was granted veteran status after being reorganized in 1864. A veteran regiment was one that had enough men reenlist to continue fighting when the unit's enlistment had expired. This veteran status often included a furlough, which could range in duration, sometimes as long as thirty days, for the men who reenlisted. Isaac received a furlough when he reenlisted (compiled military service record, Isaac Walters, Pvt., Co. F, 20 Ind. Inf.; Civil War, RG 94; NA-Washington).

21. *Congestive fever* was a period term for malaria.

22. The letter (1991.0291.55) was written in blue ink on blue-lined stationery embossed with a paper manufacturer's mark. A matching envelope has not been identified.

23. The Army of the Cumberland, originally named the Army of Ohio, was the main Union army located in the Western Theater of the war. Major General William S. Rosecrans changed the name to the Army of the Cumberland when he took command of the force in October 1862. Rosecrans was replaced after his defeat at the Battle of Chickamauga, September 18–20, 1863, by Major General George H. Thomas, who was in command at the time of this letter.

24. David Walters was referring to his wife, Rachel's, questions in her letter (1991.0291.55) dated April 6, 1864, about an overcoat.

25. John S. Louderback, from Fulton, Indiana, was serving as quartermaster sergeant at the time of this letter (Goodspeed Brothers, *Pictorial and Biographical Record*, 150–151).

26. This was a reference to the letter dated April 6, 1864 (1991.0291.55), that David Walters received from his sister-in-law Phebe A. (Ward) Dunkin.

27. The envelope (1991.0291.36) for this letter (1991.0291.35) was postmarked "PARIS / KY / APR / 12 / 64" over a three-cent George Washington stamp placed in the left corner, and a "Due 6" mark is written across the top, indicating additional postage was required for weighing over a half ounce but less than one ounce, and so assessed three cents due for the second step in weight and a three-cent penalty for insufficient postage. It was addressed "Mrs David. W. Walters / Star City Post / Pulaski Co / Ind." The letter was written on stationery embossed with a paper manufacturer's mark.

28. The referenced letter, dated April 2, is not in the collection.

29. The referenced letter from John Wesley Walters describing his movements in Louisiana is not in the collection, but an envelope (1991.0291.154) that likely contained that letter is. The envelope has two one-cent Benjamin Franklin stamps (residue from a missing third stamp is evident) placed in the upper left corner. It was postmarked "NEW ORLEANS / LA / MAR / 31 / '64" and was addressed to "Mrs. Rachel. J. Walters / Star City / Pulaski County / Indiana."

30. Shreveport, Louisiana.

31. The letter (1991.0291.56) was written in blue ink on blue-lined stationery embossed with a paper manufacturer's mark. A matching envelope has not been identified.

32. Resistance to conscription sometimes resulted in efforts to interrupt the draft by intimidating officers in charge of the draft or destroying the equipment needed to conduct it. David Walters's unit may have provided protection or been deployed to round up the conscripted men.

33. Nicholasville, Kentucky, is about thirty miles west of Winchester.

34. The envelope (1991.0291.38) for this letter (1991.0291.37) was postmarked "WINC[HES]TER / KY / APR 18" over a three-cent George Washington stamp placed on the left. It was addressed "Mrs David W / Walters Starcity / Ind." A pencil notation, "1864," and blue ink notation, "from David," were added, likely by a family member, after the letter was received and before it was donated to the museum. The letter is written on stationery embossed with a paper manufacturer's mark.

35. David Walters's letter of April 12 (1991.0291.35) is part of the collection, but the referenced letter dated April 10 is not.

36. Rachel Walters was likely describing a photograph of her husband, David, on a horse.

37. The coat was discussed in Rachel Walters's letter of April 6, 1864, and David Walters's letter of April 12, 1864.

38. This was a reference to having a photograph taken.

39. As a postscript, the abbreviation N.B., for the Latin phrase *nota bene*, or "note well," marked attention to additional or significant information. The letter

(1991.0291.57) was written in blue ink on blue-lined stationery embossed with a paper manufacturer's mark. A matching envelope has not been identified.

40. This letter was largely a direct response to Rachel Walters's letter of April 18, 1864, (1991.0291.57), which included a description of her son, Willard's, photograph.

41. David Walters imitated his wife, Rachel's, use of *N.B.* in her letter of April 18, 1864, and his lengthy notation and unusually colorful language demonstrate his strong emotions.

42. The envelope (1991.0291.40) for this letter (1991.0291.39) was postmarked "NICHOLASVILLE / KY / APR / 27 / '64" over a three-cent George Washington stamp, and a "DUE 6" handstamp applied across the top indicated additional postage was required for weighing over a half ounce but less than one ounce, and so assessed three cents due for the second step in weight and a three-cent penalty for insufficient postage. It was addressed "Mrs David. W. Walters / Starcity / Ind." The letter was written in ink on stationery embossed "E.H. Owen."

43. Rachel Walters directly responded to her husband, David's, April 26, 1864, letter (1991.0291.39) with a discussion of adequate clothing and footwear; however, her notation about letters received indicates there may have been another letter from David in this timeframe that is not in the collection.

44. The letter (1991.0291.58) was written in blue ink on blue-lined paper. A matching envelope has not been identified.

45. The referenced letter, dated May 9, is not in the collection.

46. *Lung fever* was a period term for pneumonia.

47. Rachel Walters was discussing the Overland Campaign in Virginia. In May 1864, Union general Ulysses S. Grant began the campaign against the forces of Confederate general Robert E. Lee to try to capture Richmond, Virginia. Rachel would have learned from newspaper accounts about the Battle of the Wilderness, fought May 5–7, 1864, during which approximately seventy thousand Union soldiers engaged forty thousand Confederate troops in dense woods north of Richmond. Fierce fighting in this rough terrain caused great confusion and misdirection among soldiers of both armies across the three days that led to approximately seventeen thousand Union and seven thousand Confederate casualties. Instead of retreating north, Grant shifted his forces south and reengaged Lee's forces at the Battle of Spotsylvania Court House, which started on May 8, 1864, and was still ongoing at the time of this letter (McPherson, *Battle Cry of Freedom*, 725–726).

48. The envelope (1991.0291.60) for this letter (1991.0291.59) was postmarked "STAR CITY / IND / MAY 16" below a cancelled three-cent George Washington stamp placed in the left corner. It was addressed "David W. Walters / 5th cavalry regiment of / Indiana volunteers Co I / Army of the Ohio." The letter

was written in blue ink on blue-lined stationery embossed with a paper manufacturer's mark.

49. This letter was likely written in the vicinity of Cassville, Cass Station,
and Cartersville, Georgia, as the Union forces moved south during the Atlanta
Campaign.

50. This referred to the Battle of Resaca, which started on May 13, 1864, with
skirmishing and grew into a full battle from May 14 to May 15, 1864.

51. Kingston, Georgia, is about twelve miles northwest of Cartersville and
sixty miles northwest of Atlanta, Georgia.

52. No official system existed to inform families of prisoners' status. Sending mail to and from prisoner-of-war camps was possible under restrictive
measures.

53. The letter (1991.0291.108) was written on blue paper. A matching envelope
has not been identified.

54. It is highly unlikely that Rachel Walters had received the May 22 letter
(1991.0291.108) written by John S. Louderback when she wrote this. The letter in
the collection with the latest date by her husband, David Walters, was written
on April 26, 1864 (1991.0291.39), almost a month before Rachel wrote this message. Some of David's correspondence, for which she accounted and to which
she responded in her letters, is not part of the collection.

55. The Overland Campaign was ongoing in Virginia at the time of this letter.

56. The letter (1991.0291.61) was written on blue-lined stationery embossed
"C.S." A matching envelope has not been identified.

57. Despite being clearly dated as "1863," Rachel Walters composed this letter
in 1864. Several details Rachel includes mark events that occurred in 1864: June
2 was a Thursday in 1864, marriage records for Milton Sellers and Susan Martin
are dated May 1864, and the military records for Joseph Walters show he died
in May 1864 (Fulton County, Indiana, Index to Marriage Records 1850–1920,
County Clerk's Records, marriage of Milton V. Sellers and Susan A. Martin
[1864]; Book B, Page 221; and, Indiana Digital Archives, "Military Records, Joseph Walters").

58. The advent of the telegraph made it possible for major news from the battlefield to make it to hometowns very quickly (Wheeler, *Mr. Lincoln's T-Mails*,
94–95). Despite the presence of reporters following armies and filing stories
from the field, the accuracy was debatable at times, especially during the chaos
of battles.

59. The envelope (1991.0291.46) for this letter (1991.0291.45) was postmarked
"STAR CITY / IND. / JUL 3" below a cancelled three-cent George Washington stamp in the upper left corner. It was addressed "David W. Walters / 5th
cavalry regiment / of Indiana volunteers / Co I. army of the / Ohio." The letter
was written on blue-lined stationery embossed "C.S."

60. This camp was likely near Cold Harbor, Virginia, as the Twentieth Indiana was taking part in the Overland Campaign.

61. Rachel Walters mentioned her brother-in-law Isaac Walters's visit home on furlough in her April 12, 1864, letter (1991.0291.56) to her husband, David.

62. Isaac Walters's cousin Joseph Walters enlisted in Company F, Twentieth Indiana on July 22, 1861. Joseph Walters's death is recorded on May 6, 1864, at the Battle of the Wilderness (Indiana Digital Archives, "Military Records, Joseph Walters"). The battle was fought about fifteen miles west of Fredericksburg, Virginia, hence Isaac's reference to the city. Rachel Walters's letters of May 23 and June 24 also discuss the news of Joseph Walters's death.

63. Despite Isaac Walters's comment about the envelope, it is unremarkable for its condition or construction. The envelope (1991.0291.89) for this letter (1991.0291.88) was postmarked "WASHINGTON / Ju[illegible] 16 [illegible]" over a three-cent George Washington stamp placed in the left corner. It is addressed "Mrs. Rachel. J. Walters / Star. City. /Pulaski. Co. / Ind." The letter was written on blue-lined stationery embossed with a paper manufacturer's mark.

64. This camp was located somewhere outside of Petersburg, Virginia, as the Twentieth Indiana participated in the siege of the city. Petersburg, just south of Richmond, was a key supply point for the Confederate army. After failing to capture the city by assault, the Union army dug in to besiege the city. Union forces made repeated assaults to capture the rail lines leading into the city and break through Confederate defenses. Isaac Walters and the Twentieth Indiana took part in numerous engagements during the summer of 1864 as the Union extended its lines to surround the city and cut off supplies to the Confederate army (McPherson, *Battle Hymn of the Republic*, 756).

65. John Wesley Walters died of disease in Royal Center, Indiana, June 28, 1864 (compiled military service record, John Wesley Walters, Pvt., Co. I, 46 Ind. Inf.; Civil War, RG 94; NA-Washington).

66. David Walters was reported captured during the Battle of Resaca in a letter sent to his wife, Rachel, by John S. Louderback dated May 22, 1864 (1991.0291.108).

67. This refers to a raid into Maryland launched by Confederate forces in June 1864. Led by General Jubal A. Early, the attack went through Maryland and approached Washington, DC, before being stopped at the Battle of Fort Stevens on July 11 and 12, 1864. It was meant to distract General Ulysses S. Grant from his campaign against the Confederate capital of Richmond, Virginia.

68. President Abraham Lincoln.

69. The letter (1991.0291.90) was written on blue-lined stationery embossed with a paper manufacturer's mark. A matching envelope has not been identified.

70. This camp was located somewhere outside of Petersburg, Virginia, as the Twentieth Indiana participated in the siege of the city.

71. *Graybacks* was a nickname for Confederate soldiers often used by Union soldiers.

72. The Petersburg Campaign was a large siege designed to capture the railroad lines and supply hub located at Petersburg, Virginia. General Ulysses Grant believed that by taking Petersburg, he could force the Confederates to abandon the capital at Richmond, Virginia.

73. James River.

74. During the August 14–20, 1864, Battle of Second Deep Bottom, part of the siege of Petersburg, Confederate brigadier general John R. Chambliss was killed, but the other details given by Isaac Walters are not accurate. For example, the Union army did not capture as many prisoners as Isaac describes, and the Union army returned to the south side of the James River on August 20, shortly after this letter was written.

75. *Jonnys*, or *Johnnys*, was a term often used by Union soldiers to describe Confederate soldiers, derived from the term *Johnny Reb*.

76. *Minnies* refers to Minié balls, which were a common type of bullet for rifles during the Civil War.

77. The letter (1991.0291.91) was written on blue-lined stationery embossed "Shepherd & Riley / Washington." A matching envelope has not been identified.

78. The Twentieth Indiana fought in the Battle of Boydton Plank Road, October 27–28, 1864, near Petersburg, Virginia. The regiment camped in the vicinity afterward as it continued to participate in the siege of the city.

79. Indiana did not pass legislation to allow military service members to vote by absentee ballot in the presidential election of 1864. At the behest of Governor Oliver Morton and President Abraham Lincoln, many soldiers were granted leave to return to their home precincts to cast their ballots (Benton, *Voting in the Field*, 291–292).

80. The envelope (1991.0291.93) for this letter (1991.0291.92) was postmarked "WASHINGTON / DC / NOV [*illegible*]" to the left of a cancelled three-cent George Washington stamp. It was addressed "Mrs. Rachel. J. Walters / Star. City. Pulaski / Co. Ind." The letter was written on blue-lined, laid paper embossed "Codorus Mills."

81. The Twentieth Indiana eventually completed winter quarters near Petersburg, Virginia, and continued to participate in the siege of that city.

82. Boone Township, Cass County, Indiana.

83. *Copperhead*, referencing the name of a poisonous snake, began as a derogatory name for Northern Democrats who opposed the war. Jennifer Weber explains in *Copperheads* that "Republicans started calling them Copperheads in the summer of 1861, when an anonymous letter-writer to the *Cincinnati Commercial* suggested this would be an apt term for Ohio's Peace Democrats, whose

motto the writer thought should be drawn from Genesis 3:14: 'Upon thy belly shalt thou go, and dust shalt thou eat all the days of thy life;'" and, some Peace Democrats refashioned the term into a positive representation of their beliefs and took to wearing modified pennies, also known as copperheads, that featured the profile of Lady Liberty (pages 2–3).

84. The envelope (1991.0291.95) for this letter (1991.0291.94) was postmarked "[WAS]HINGTON / [*illegible*]" to the left of a cancelled three-cent George Washington stamp. It was addressed "Mrs. Rachel. J. Walters / Star. City / Pulaski. Co / Ind." The letter was written in blue ink on blue-lined stationery embossed with a paper manufacturer's mark.

85. The Twentieth Indiana spent the winter of 1864 in the trenches outside Petersburg, Virginia, continuing the siege of the city.

86. There are no letters in the collection by David during his internment as a prisoner of war.

87. Gouverneur K. Warren started the war as a lieutenant colonel of the Fifth New York and was promoted to the rank of major general. Warren was assigned to command the V Corps shortly before the start of the Overland Campaign and still held the command at the time of this letter. The raid described is the Stony Creek Raid, also known as the Hicksford Raid, which occurred from December 7 to December 12, 1864, and destroyed miles of the vital Weldon rail line. As Noah Andre Trudeau explains in his work *The Last Citadel*, "The orders went out to begin tearing up the Weldon line. 'First the rails were removed,' a soldier in the 32nd Massachusetts wrote, 'then the sleepers were taken up, piled and fired; when the rails, laid across the burning ties, were heated as to be pliable, they were doubled and twisted in such manner that they could not be relaid unless rerolled. Then the same operation was repeated on another length of track until several miles in all were ruined. It was a long days work'" (page 271).

88. General William T. Sherman started the war as a colonel in the US Army. He served in the Western Theater as commander of the Union armies in Georgia and successfully carried out the campaign in 1864 that led to the fall of Atlanta and Savannah as the Union army moved across the state from the northwest to the southeast.

89. The fall of Savannah occurred on December 21, 1864. The Union army succeeded in capturing some ammunition and equipment, but, regardless of Isaac Walters's description, relatively few Confederate soldiers were captured as a majority of Confederate forces retreated into South Carolina.

90. The envelope (1991.0291.97) for this letter (1991.0291.96) was postmarked "WASHINGTON / D.C. / DEC 24" over a three-cent George Washington stamp. It was addressed "Rachel J Walters / Star City / Pulaski Co / Ind." The letter was written in blue ink on blue-lined paper.

—⟋⟍—

FIVE

1865 AND THE POSTWAR YEARS

In haste I drop you a few lines in answer to yours bearing date of
July 12th which is before me, and as I see you have misunderstood
the name I wish to have it corrected. I see that you have
it Daniel W. Walters instead of David W. Walters.

—Rachel J. Walters to Clara Barton, July 21, 1866

IN A RELATIVELY QUIET PERIOD, Isaac Walters wrote to his sister-in-law
Rachel Walters on January 10, 1865, from his regiment's winter quarters outside
of Petersburg, Virginia. The campaign resumed in February with combat that
successfully enabled the Union forces to continue extending their lines around
the city. Confederate general Robert E. Lee knew that his army could not stand
the siege for much longer and drew up an audacious plan for a surprise attack
on Fort Stedman in the early morning of March 25, 1865. Despite the success of
the Confederate forces at the fort, this was one of their last offensive maneuvers.
Their ability to wage war had waned greatly since the loss of Atlanta in July 1864
had cut off supply lines to the Army of Northern Virginia. Union forces soon
took back the lost ground in and around Fort Stedman, and General Ulysses S.
Grant regrouped his troops to launch massive attacks on April 1 and 2 that finally
broke through the Confederate lines. Following the capture of Petersburg, Lee
alerted Confederate president Jefferson Davis, and military units and members
of the government evacuated the capital at Richmond, Virginia. Lee's army fled
west, hoping to find supplies and to join additional troops en route to Virginia
from North Carolina. Grant and his forces caught up to them outside of Appomattox Court House, where Lee surrendered the Army of Northern Virginia
on April 9, 1865. Although the surrender did not mark the end of the conflict, it
signaled to many that the war was quickly reaching its end.[1]

Recollections of the prisoner-of-war camp near Florence, South Carolina, were depicted in *Counting Us Off* and other watercolors by James E. Taylor. In 1897, veteran Ezra Hoyt Ripple commissioned Taylor to illustrate his lecture series on the war and his experiences as a POW in the Andersonville Prison and Florence Stockade. Many did not survive the overcrowded and inhumane conditions in POW camps, including David W. Walters, who reportedly suffered starvation and died in Florence, South Carolina, in February 1865. *(Library of Congress, LC-USZ62-121343)*

Only three letters from Isaac to his sister-in-law Rachel exist from the period of the final campaign. The Twentieth Indiana participated in months of hard fighting to take Petersburg and in the final battles near Appomattox Court House. On April 17, 1865, Isaac wrote to Rachel as he processed the shocking news of the assassination of President Abraham Lincoln just two days prior. Death pervades this missive, and Isaac reflects on the war and its toll: "It has pleased the Almighty to Spare my life & bring me Safely through the last Struggle while many have breathed their last on the Field of Battle & in their horrible

Sign for the Missing Soldiers Office, 7th Street, NW, Washington, DC. At this site, Clara Barton operated the Office of Correspondence with the Friends of the Missing Men of the United States Army. In 1866, Rachel J. Walters corresponded with the Missing Soldiers Office so she could assemble the information necessary to complete a widow's pension application. *(Courtesy of US General Services Administration, image provided by National Museum of Civil War Medicine)*

Prisons in the South which I think is the worst of all Deaths." His pity for prisoners of war included his brother David, who had been captured in May 1864. Isaac went on to lament, "I hope he has gone where war & Starvation will never come nor Sickness nor Death." In his February 19, 1865, letter, Isaac comments that he was "glad to hear from David," but by his April letter, the optimism that Isaac had expressed previously had vanished; the fateful news of his brother's death must have reached him. The family received confirmation of their worst fears for David when Captain John S. Louderback wrote to Rachel Walters on May 27, 1865.

The sincere condolence message from John Louderback, written while the Fifth Indiana Cavalry prepared to muster out, also informed Rachel that she was entitled to her husband's pension and the money due him. According to Louderback, the paperwork on the status of David Walters would not be completed by him for Company I, Fifth Indiana; instead "Davids name will be perhaps transfered to an other Company untill such thimes as there can be some orders from the War Department to Dispose of those that cannt now be accounted for." The ramifications of the incomplete status shaped Rachel's life over the following years as she sought evidence of David's death during his time in military service.

During the war, the US Congress passed legislation to ensure federal pensions for those Union soldiers wounded in battle as well as for the widows and children of service members who died on duty.[2] Numerous laws introduced after the war, however, created a maze of bureaucracy in the pension system that veterans and their families had to navigate. The concept of pensions for military service was not new—the Federal Pension Act of 1818 provided funds for veterans of the Revolutionary War, and the government made pensions available to veterans of the War of 1812 and the Mexican-American War. The number of pensions needed after the Civil War, however, caused many politicians and civilians to reassess and seek justification for the cost of the pension system. The process became rigorous and onerous for veterans and their dependents to complete. The pension laws required that veterans, not the government, must collect all identification and evidence, such as statements from those who witnessed the claimant's injury or from a doctor who may have treated wounds in the field. Obtaining such documentation, especially after the war, could be extremely difficult or impossible if an individual had passed away. Rachel Walters found herself in this situation as a widow with a child to raise.

In a letter dated April 26, 1866, Rachel asked John S. Louderback, her husband's former commanding officer, to provide information needed to "draw a pension and the bounty and back pay that was due my husband." Meanwhile, she obtained affidavits from witnesses to her marriage to David and to the birth of their son, Willard.[3] Among those affidavits in the official pension files stored at the National Archives is testimony from veteran George W. Stalnaker, who stated to the Pulaski County clerk on June 19, 1866, that he witnessed David suffering from starvation at the prisoner-of-war camp in Florence, South Carolina.[4] About the same time of Stalnaker's official statement, Rachel arranged to have her husband's name included on the rolls published by the Missing Soldiers Office. Founded by Clara Barton, the Office of Correspondence with the Friends of the Missing Men of the United States Army solicited the public to send in inquiries and answers about service members who remained unaccounted for at the war's end. Barton and a small staff collected names, like that of David Walters, and sent them to newspapers across the country in hopes that veterans would reply with information about the last known whereabouts of the missing. Family and friends turned to this office for help when they did not know whether their loved ones had died, fallen ill, or chosen not to return. Over the course of its short but intense operations from 1865 to 1868, the office sent 63,182 letters of inquiry, wrote 41,855 personal letters, and identified 22,000 missing men.[5] Unlike the thousands writing with inquiries to the Missing Soldiers Office, Rachel knew the circumstances of her husband's death. Her use of the correspondence service was atypical; she sought verification in order to secure a pension.[6] In early 1867, the Missing Soldiers Office sent Rachel Walters two differing accounts from veterans Russell P. Finney and John Brown. Rachel heard again from John Louderback when, on January 17, 1867, he relayed information from George McKinsey, another member of Company I, who had seen David's body at the Florence Stockade. Being confronted again and again with accounts of her husband's death required Rachel's emotional fortitude as well as commitment, time, and finances—including the cost of mail—while she strove to amass the information necessary to complete the paperwork for a pension.

In addition to seeking assistance from the Missing Soldiers Office, Rachel experienced more changes in her correspondence network. Of the letters sent by Isaac Walters, the one with the latest date in the collection was written on May 19, 1865. Combat was over, the Twentieth Indiana mustered out in July, and Isaac returned to Indiana. Nevertheless, during the postwar years, Rachel received and kept letters from other family members: her sisters-in-law, Emmaline and Martha Walters, and father-in-law, John Walters.

Such correspondence sustained Rachel's connections and, importantly, enabled her to secure a widow's pension to support herself and her son. Records show that she received payment on September 4, 1868. She died shortly thereafter on December 15, 1868—the pension paperwork included Rachel's date of death but no cause.[7] Rachel's death left Willard an orphan, a situation faced by many children as a result of the war. The death toll of the Civil War created a crisis of children left parentless.[8] Church organizations and philanthropic groups responded by opening new orphanages throughout the country to handle the increased need. Private committees established by citizens in numerous states, both North and South, raised much-needed funds to help pay for the care of the war's orphans. Many state governments also opened state-funded homes or took over private institutions when funds ran low. James Marten described the crisis and response within Indiana, where orphaned children "originally lived in the state-sponsored soldiers' home, until then numbers overwhelmed those of the disabled veterans and a separate institution was established in 1870."[9] Despite the terrible situation created by the deaths of both his parents, Willard Walters had advantages over others orphaned by the war because he had his maternal grandparents as his guardians, and they worked to secure the pension in his name. As late as 1880, and no longer a minor, Willard still faced beneficiary issues when he received correspondence from a "Pension Claims and Collections Specialist."[10] The war's aftermath had shifted the reasons for and makeup of the families' correspondence networks, a reflection of the even greater changes it wrought in the lives of the Walters and Ward families.

ISAAC WALTERS TO RACHEL J. WALTERS

Camp of the 20th Ind[11]
Jan 10th/ 65

Dear Sister

I this morning Compose myself in order to Answer your very kind & welcome letter Dated Dec 21 which came to hand last night & was read with much Interest. I was very glad to hear from you once more & hear that you are well. I hope you may Still be permitted to enjoy this good blessing. My health at the present time is not very good. I have been Sick for about two weeks withe the Fever   I have the fever broke & am Improving every day but my nerves are very weak yet as you will See by my writing I can hardy write alot. I am glad to hear you are going to School & trying to Improve your education. I am Sorry to hear that you dont get any word from David any more   I dont See the reason   I would think they would let the boys write to their Friends. well Rachel I think the war will Soon be over then we can all return home feeling Setesfied & contented knowing that we have done our duty with reference to our Country our fellow man & our Selves I think we ought to die contented & happy.

we had rather a gloomy newyears here   nothing going on to enliven the Scene a lot   how was it there with you. to it rains very hard & is getting very Muddy   Some early thunder. all things are quiet along the front lines & have been for some time   no firing along the lines where we do duty   well rachel as I have nothing of much Interest to write this time & dont feel very well for writing I will bring my letter to a close hoping you will overlook & excuse my poor Composition & poor writing & write Soon again with many wishes for your property & happiness

I bid you good bye
Isaac Walters[12]

Fortifications in front of Petersburg, Virginia, 1865. Isaac Walters sent a few letters to his sister-in-law Rachel from the Twentieth Indiana's positions during the siege. *(Library of Congress, LC-DIG-cwpb-01326)*

ISAAC WALTERS TO RACHEL J. WALTERS

Camp of the 20th Ind Vet Vols[13]
Feb 19th /65

Dear Sister

I now compose myself in order to Answer your most kind &truly welcome letter Dated the 3rd which came to hand Several days ago but I have been So busy I could not write until this morning. your letter found me well & I trust this will find you the Same. I was glad to receive a letter from your hand once more & learn that you Still enjoy good health. I hope this kind blessing may Still be extended toward you. I am glad to hear from David.[14] it is not only a great consolation to you but all his Friends. I hope his life may be Spared to return home to his Friends & we may be permitted to enjoy each others Company many long days that are yet in the Future   I often think of him & wonder how he is getting along to day or to night & where he is, what he has to eat & to wear how he is treated & my heart cries for our poor unfortunate prisoners. I believe I would prefer Death to being taken Prisoner at this time   I think Death would be sweet Compared with their Suffering   I never will be taken Prisoner while I can Fight or run. & I dont propose to run unless I am overpowered. there is a man that had 5 balls put through his body by a lot of Guerillas the time of the raid on the Weldon Railroad who is getting well. He belongs to our regt. he was attacked by 3 men   he killed two of them & one of their horses. & was overpowered but fought till the last & left for ded by the Enemy who fled & made their escape. he was close to the road & was discovered by Some of our own men who Saw there was Still life in him & brought off &Sent to the Hospital. he is now nearly well. Such Soldiers Should be honored by all who live to know them. well Rachel you need not be Surprised if you Should See me in old Ind[15] before long   I have Applied for a Furlough & I think it will be Approved   I hope we will have a good time if I am So lucky as to get there. I will close for this time & hope you will write soon Again

Yours as ever
Isaac Walters[16]

ISAAC WALTERS TO RACHEL J. WALTERS

Camp in the Field V.A.

Aprile 17th/ 65[17]

Dear Absent Sister & Friends

I am happy to Say to you to day that my life & health is Spared to
See the close of this cruel war[18] which has brought So many of the
braver Sons of the North to their graves it has pleased the Almighty
to Spare my life & bring me Safely through the last Struggle while
many have breathed their last on the Field of Battle & in their horrible
Prisons in the South which I think is the worst of all Deaths   I
would ten times rather be killed in battle than die there in Filth & dirt
with Starvation   This is horrible in the extrem to think of let lone
to Suffer as those poor Soldiers have done   thanks be to the name
of him who has guided & protected me through this awful rebellion.
but Alas! for my poor brother who has fallen a victim to their cruel
hands. Oh! what a Sickening thought that Such a near Friend Should
perish in Such a way & Such a place as one of those Southern Prisons
are represented to be. it Seems as though I never could get over it in the
world. I know I never can forgive them for their wicked deeds while I
live   when I was home it Seemed to to me that I never would See
David any more   Something Seemed to tell me So but of course I
wouldnt tell you So for I thought you had trouble enough without me
causing you more. but I hope he is better off than we are   I hope
he has gone where war & Starvation will never come nor Sickness
nor Death but where he can Sing Songs of praise to God & the Holy
Angels forever & ever. I hope we Shall one day meet him in that bright
clime never to part again. I hope that we may live So that we will meet
with the kind approbation. Enter in to my joys & Sit down on my
throne. we are now lying on the Railroad running from Petersburg to
Lynchburg about 55 miles from Petersburg   I think we are Staying
here waiting for the roads to dry & become good   then I think we
will be Sent to washington or Some place to do garrison duty   there
are many rumors afloat about where we are going & what we are going
to do but nothing that can be relied on as true. we will have to wait
with patience until things are further developed before we can tell
what will be done but I hope I Shall See home in the course of a few
months   Yesterday we received Intelligence that Abe Lincoln

Secretary Seward & his Son were all Assassinated.[19] This is awful if
true but I hope it is not   if this is true it is very likely we will be held
5 or 6 months longer than we would have been   otherwise I close
for the present hoping Soon to get an Answer   remaining as Ever

your Sincere Friend
Isaac Walters[20]

ISAAC WALTERS TO RACHEL J. WALTERS

Washington City[21]
Camp of the 20th Ind. Vols Near
May 19th /65

Dear Sister

This Morning I am Seated to answer Your kind & most excellent
letter Dated May the 11th which came to hand on the 17th & found me
enjoying good health. Rachel I can truly say I was glad to hear from
you once more & learn that you are well. I am very sorry you have met
with your great loss & feel to mourn with you but I hope our loss may
prove his great gain. it is very hard to loose a near friend in the way we
lost him. I would not feel half So bad if he had been killed in battle as
to have died as he did.[22] I wish I could have heared his funeral Sermon.
I think he took a very appropriate text & a very nice one. I think if ably
handled it must have been a very nice Sermon   well rachel our
long & tiresome march is over. we arrived here on the 15th this month.
was 15 days marching through from Birks Station V.A.[23] we had Some
pretty bad roads to march over & Some pretty warm weather but the
most of the troops Stood it very well. there ware Some died of course
as there are always more or less die on all long marches. but none I
believe in our own Regiment but you must recollect we are Hoosers &
they are tuffer than our Army beef & that is tuffer than whalebone. we
are lying here waiting for Shermans Army to get up here & get rested
then we are going to have a big review the 20th of this month was Set
apart for that purpose but it is now deffered until the 23rd & 24th / the
army of the Potomac will be reviewed the first day & Shermans on the
Second[24]   when this is over then I think the Soldiers will Start for
their homes in the north. or many of them at least. I think perhaps the
Veteran Soldiers may retained in Service for a while but I think not
long. they cant discharge me any to Soon for I am tired of Soldiering
& am very anxious to get home. I want to change my mode of living. I
think it would be rather agreeable at least I am very willing to try it. I
wish you could be here to witness our review I think you would enjoy
yourself very well. I think it would relieve your mind from trouble it
is going to be a hard job for the Soldiers but very pleasant for lookers
on   I expect many of us will behold the light of day for the last time
on those two days Especially if it is very warm weather. We marched
in the view through Richmond & there were a good many put off their

US infantry troops paraded in the Grand Review on May 23 and May 24, 1865, to celebrate the victorious Union armies. Isaac Walters was preparing to take part when he wrote about his regiment's plans in his May 19, 1865, letter to his sister-in-law Rachel. *(Library of Congress, LC-B8171-3314)*

feet never to rise again. a person unacquainted with those marches would think this very strange & almost Impossible but it is never the less true. Well Rachel I believe I have nothing more to Communicate at this time. So I will close by wishing you well Write Soon again

Yours with true regard
Isaac Walters[25]

Before the men of the Fifth Indiana Cavalry prepared to muster out in the spring of 1865, they strove to complete their personal correspondence and paperwork. Captain John S. Louderback had the solemn duty to write on May 27, 1865, to inform Rachel J. Walters that her husband, David, had died in February while being held as a prisoner of war. (*National Postal Museum, Smithsonian Institution, 1991.0291.109*)

his final Statements yet & Cannot do so till
Some one file an Affidavit of his death

I will do all that I can in Shapeing his
affares here So that you can get his Paws
you will be Entitled to a Pension as his
disease was contracted while in Division

There is a tin Case at my House that you
Can get that belongs to his by Calling there

I am now Repareing the muster out Roll
of the Company whose thime Expires before the
first Day of Oct Davids name will be perhaps
transfered to an other Company un till such
thime as there can be Some orders from the
War Department to Dispose of those that
Cant now be accounted for

any information that I can give
yo I will redily do it for your adconada
ion You can address me at this Place or at
My Home as you like
          Yours with Respect

          John A Sauterback
          Capt Co I 5th Ind Cav

JOHN S. LOUDERBACK TO RACHEL J. WALTERS

Camp 5th Ind Cav
Pulaski Tenn May 27th 1865
Misses Walters
Starr City Pulaski Co Ind

Be not weary or troubled   Trust in the Lord for he is able to Comfort

I think I am Safe in Saying that your Husband D W Walters Died in Reble Prision about the 10th of Febuary   I Saw him a bout the 5th   he was then unable to help him self   I waited on him & gave him as much Comfort as I could untill I was taken down my Self   He often Spoke of you & his little Boy Whitch he Spoke of with a greateal of Respect & Seemed to waiting with a greateal of anxziety for the thime to Come when the Prision doores would be thrown open that he could return to his loved ones at home but alas the Small amount of Meal that he was allowed was not Suffitient for him   I did not se him Dye my self but I have bin told by Competen Persons that he Died a bout the thime that I have Stated

I think that David had experienced a a Chang & that he was endevering to live the life of a Christian   He was one of my best men & I felt vairy Sorry to here of his Death   I have not Made out his final Statements yet & Cannot do so till Some one files an Affidavit of his death

I will do all that I can in Shapeing has affares here So that you can get his Dews   You will be Entitled to a Pension as his Diseas was contracted while in Prision   There is a tin Cace at my House that you Can get that belongs to him by Calling there[26]

I am now Prepareing the muster out Rolls of the Company whoos thime Expires before the first Day of Oct   Davids name will be perhaps transfered to an other Company untill such thimes as there can be some orders from the War Department to Dispose of those that cannt now be accounted for

any information that I can give you I will redily do it for your accomadasion   You can address me at this Place or at My Home as you like

Yours with Respect
John S Louderback
Capt Co I 5th Ind Cav[27]

RACHEL J. WALTERS TO JOHN S. LOUDERBACK

Winamac Ind
Apr. 26th 1866

Mr. John S Louderback
Dear Sir

    after my respects to you I would say that I am reasonably well and sincerely hope these lines may find you and yours enjoying good health and a degree of happiness. My object in writing this morning is this, I had papers fixed out last May in order that I might draw a pension and the bounty and back pay that was due my husband. I have not heard any thing from them since until yesterday my employer Mr. G. F. Wickersham showed me a letter which he has received a few days ago, stating that they could not close up the business until I should get evidence of my husbands death. also the date of the same[28]   If you can give me any information concerning it or of any person or persons that can you will confer a great favor on me by so doing

    hoping to hear from you soon, I close

yours with due respect
Rachel J. Walters

Please address
Mrs R J. Walters
Winamac
Pulaski Co
Ind
Box No. 107[29]

Clara Barton's Missing Soldiers Office to Rachel J. Walters

[Printed stationery. The blanks completed in handwriting are underlined.]

Office of Correspondence
for Missing Men of the U.S. Army,
Washington, <u>12 July 1865</u>.6

Dear <u>Madam</u>

Your communication of <u>*[Blank line is struck through.]*</u> is received, and the name of <u>Daniel W. Walters, I 5 Ind Cavy will be</u> placed upon my lists. It will be my earnest endeavor to bring these lists to the notice of returned soldiers everywhere.

Be assured that as soon as any information of interest to you is gained, it will be promptly forwarded.

Very sincerely yours,
[handwritten] Clara Barton
[handwritten] per@[30]

Facing, Rachel J. Walters's letter of July 21, 1866, asked Clara Barton's Missing Soldiers Office to correct the name of her deceased husband for the organization's rolls that were published to solicit information about men missing at the war's end. *(National Postal Museum, Smithsonian Institution, 1991.0291.64)*

Winamac Ind
July 21st 1866

Miss Clara Barton
                Dear Madam

                              In haste I
drop you a few lines in answer
to yours bearing date of July
18th which is before me.

                and as I see you have
misunderstood the name I wish
to have it corrected. I see that
you have it Samuel W. Walters
instead of David W. Walters

                        please correct it before
having it placed up on your
lists it is. David W. Walters Co
I 5th Ind cavy

                              Very sincerely yours

                              Rachel J. Walters

Rachel J. Walters and Clara Barton Correspondence

Winamac Ind
July 21st 1866

Miss Clara Barton
Dear Madam

     In haste I drop you a few lines in answer to yours bearing date of July 12th[31] which is before me, and as I see you have misunderstood the name I wish to have it corrected. I see that you have it Daniel W. Walters instead of David W. Walters.
     please correct it before having it placed upon your lists   it is David W.Walters Co I 5th Ind Cavy

Very sincerely yours,
Rachel J Walters

[Message on the back of the sheet is in a different handwriting and ink.]

The name is corrected to
David. W. Walters
I 5th Ind Cay

Very Truly Yours
Clara Barton
pera

W_ D.C
Oct 16 66[32]

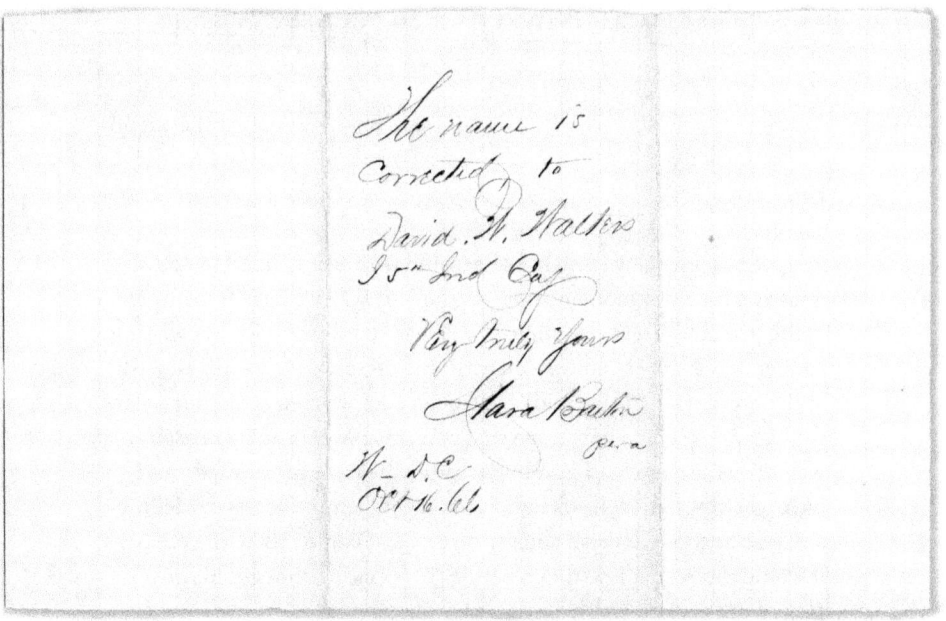

On October 16, 1866, a Missing Soldiers Office staff member responded on the back of Rachel J. Walters's July 21 letter to confirm that the name of David W. Walters was corrected in the rolls. *(National Postal Museum, Smithsonian Institution, 1991.0291.64)*

EMMA AND MATTIE [WALTERS] TO RACHEL J. WALTERS

A I Ohio[33]

August the 9 1866

Dear sister[34]

After a long delay i find my self seated with pen in hand to converse
with you for a few moments for it is the only way we have to converse
at the present [*illegible deletion*]   Please pardon me for not writing
sooner   I have been very busy till the present   we are all well
at the present   Isaac and I have been complaining some but we are
well now   I cincerely hope that you are all well. i enjoy my self verry
well this summer   I go a buggy riding nearly evry sunday   i
have gay times, my fellows name is Marvin Dennis. he is a gay fellow
a good boy too. I do wish you was here   i could talk with you.
it would interest you so much better   Isaac has not got his girl
picked out yet i guess. we have plenty of company   we do not get
lonesome   Mattie injoys her self verry well   there isent hardly a
day but what some body calls to see us   Cousin Virgil and his wife
has been to see us since Mattie is here   they injoyed them selves
verry much   i was not at home   I was out a riding   i would
have injoyed there company very much   well i guess i will close for
the present and go and get supper   please excuse [*illegible deletion*]
my short letter   i must give way for mattie   i am going away to
visit a lady frieng this evening   i have most 3 miles to go   i will
stay all night   i must hurry   it is 4 oclock now so good by from

Emma

to Rachel

[*Correspondence by Mattie Walters continues on the same sheet.*]

Dear Sister

no doubt you think it a long time to wait for a letter but you will have
the kindness to forgive when I tell you how busy I have been ever Since
I came and when I could have written on Sabbath we had company.
This is a pleasant place and very thickly Settled   Father lives on

the main public road which makes the place more pleasant than many countrey homes   I enjoy myself better than I anticipated yet I feel almost forsaken and when I reflect over my past life I cannot think why I have thus lived. I have been but little comfort to any one as far as I can understand and Oh what misery I have endured   tongues cannot tell nor pen portray. I trust in God for future happiness   I think I have Suffered enough for one life.

You Spoke in you letter of being so lonely   I Sympathize with you   I know from Sad experience how to pity your lonely condition but Dear Sister look to the future with bright with anticipation   You will not always have to Suffer. I wish you was near me   we would try to be a Source of comfort to each other in Our deep trouble. there is a Sweet consolation intermingling with your Sorrow that I am bereft of   that of meeting with your Dear companion in the full enjoyment of peace on that peaceful Shore where all loved ones meet   but my own Situation Oh I cannot dwell upon it or it will drive me mad. I fear I shal loase my right mind yet I am not my self any more   I never was so thin in flesh before as I be now. I would not grieve if I could avoid it but cannot I know   I cannot make matters any better   would to God I could   I hear Scandallous reports from [illegible] which makes me feel worse but it is no more than I expected. well I will close this Subject asking you to tell me all you may hear in regard to it. I might has been writing you how well Isaac & Father were getting along and how well every thing looks but my trouble is uppermost in my mind and is hard to quell.

I was somewhat Surprised to hear of Phebe being married but hope She has a kind companion.[35] if they should move to the point you mentioned that is near Ft Waine[36] & more than half way here   So we can expect you to visit us   I hope you can Soon

Well I must close this for the present hopeing you will not delay writing because I have been so long about it. I hope I Shall have more time now that we have things straightened up.

When you write dont fail to give me all particulars of importance & I will do the Same. excuse us for not writing more kiss Willie for me and accept my love   you can direct to Ema

good by   your friend Mattie

[Postscript continues in the top margin of the first page.]

ill send you one of isaacs photos   it is soiled some
but it is the onely one that he has now   he has not
got any to ben yet but when he gets some to ben you
can have one[37]

JOHN S. LOUDERBACK TO RACHEL J. WALTERS

Valparaiso
Jan 17th 1867

Miss Rachel Walters
Star City Ind

I learned a short thime ago by George McKinsey[38] of my Company that he saw your Husband D Walters Lying ded at the Prision gate as he passed at of the Prision at Florenc S.C. This will enable you to get his back pay Bounty & Pension which you had art to a had long ago

Have your attorney make out the propper papers & send them to me & I will attend to it for you

Mr McKinsey lives at Wheeler & it may be some dlay in seeing him

I remain vairy
Respectfully your Obt servt
John S. Louderback
Late Capt. Co. I   5th Ind Cav[39]

RUSSELL P. FINNEY TO CLARA BARTON

[Handwritten correspondence on stationery with printed letterhead.
The date blank completed in handwriting is underlined.]

Office of R. P. Finney,[40]
(Late Maj. 6th Ind. Cav.)

Attorney for all Classes of
Army and Navy Claims,
No. 33 Main Street.
Richmond, <u>Feb. 27th</u> 18<u>67</u>,
Ind.

Miss Clara Barton,
Washington D.C.

Dear Madam

    I write to procure one copy of each No. of "Roll of Missing Men"
except No 5 which I have.
    Walters David W. "I" Co. 5th Ina Cav. (No 5) was evidently Killed
by the enemy at Resaca, Ga. on 14th day of May 1864. I saw him just a
moment before he was taken prisoner. he was sitting by the side of a log
corn crib having lost his horse he gave out while we were retreating.
As I passed him I said to him, David catch one of these loose Horses
and You can make Your escape. he made no effort to do so, and from
the fact of the enemy being close at hand, and two or three men of my
Company who were taken prisoners at the same place, but a short time
before returned to th command. they report that <u>Walters,</u> was never
heard of after the fight.

Very Truly
R. P. Finney

[Message on the back of the sheet is in a different handwriting and ink.]

This is all the information I have received thus far
Clara Barton
W_D C
2 Mch 67 / Clara Barton[41]

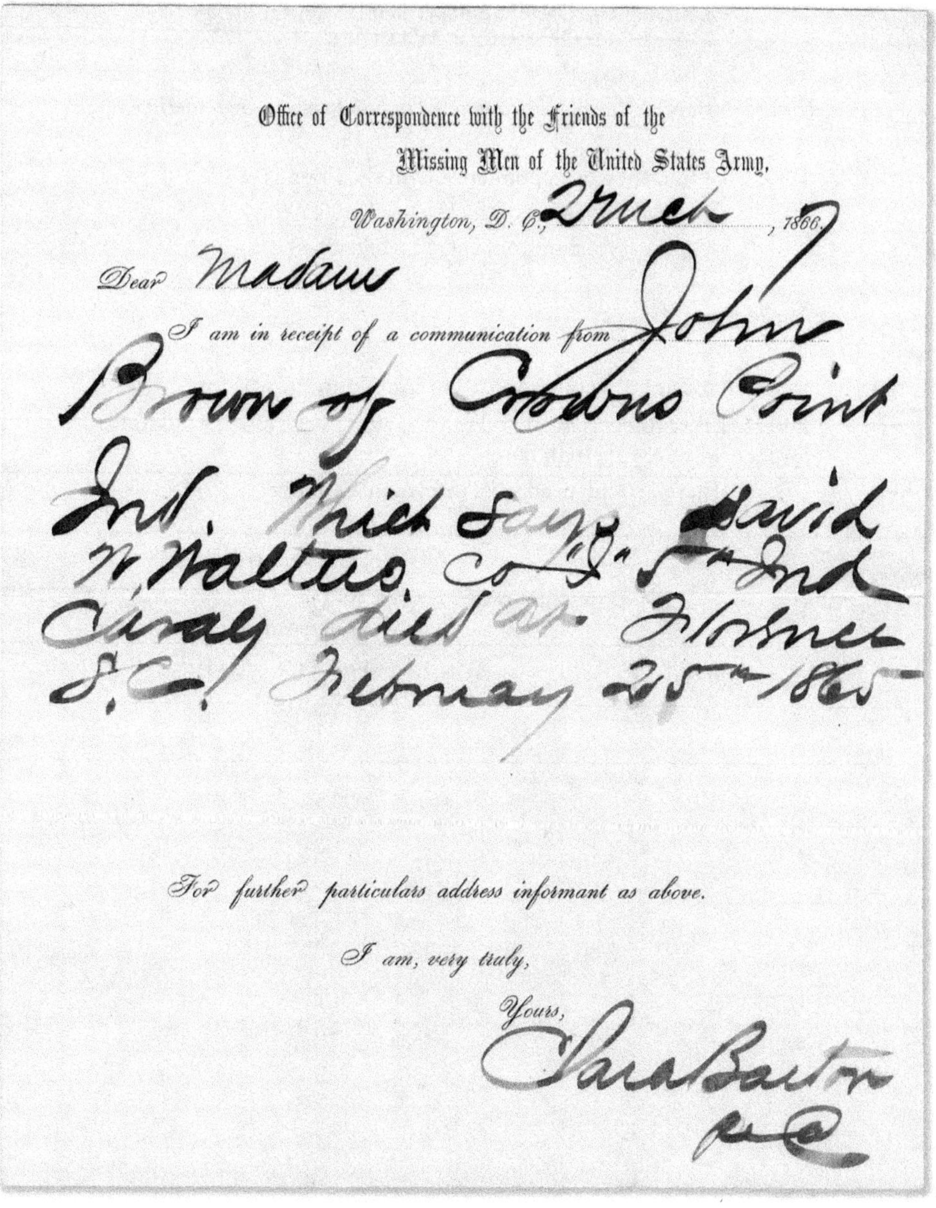
Office of Correspondence with the Friends of the
Missing Men of the United States Army,

Washington, D. C., 2 March, 1867

Dear Madam

I am in receipt of a communication from John Brown of Crowns Point Ind. which says David N. Walters Co "I" 5th Ind Cavaly died at Florence S.C. February 25th 1865

For further particulars address informant as above.

I am, very truly,

Yours,

Clara Barton
per C.

The statement sent by Clara Barton's Missing Soldiers Office on March 2, 1867, to Rachel J. Walters contained information about the death of her husband, David, as reported by army veteran John Brown. *(National Postal Museum, Smithsonian Institution, 1991.0291.134)*

CLARA BARTON'S MISSING SOLDIERS OFFICE
TO RACHEL J. WALTERS

[Printed stationery. The blanks completed in handwriting are underlined.]

Office of Correspondence with the Friends of the
Missing Men of the United States Army,
Washington, D.C., <u>2 Mch</u>, 1866<u>7</u>

Dear <u>Madam</u>

    I am in receipt of a communication from <u>John Brown</u>[42] <u>of Crowns
Point Ind. Which says David W. Walters Co "I" 5th Ind Cavay died at
Florence S.C. Februay 25th 1865</u>
    For further particulars address informant as above.

I am, very truly,
Yours,
[handwritten] Clara Barton
[handwritten] p@[43]

JOHN WALTERS TO RACHEL J. WALTERS

Ai Fulton Co Ohio
Oct 28 1868

Mrs Rachel Dear Daughter and Family

I have the opportunity of writing to you once more to let you know we are all alive & well and I hope when this reaches you that you & yours may be enjoying good health and happiness   it has been a long time Since you wrote to us   if we had have known your address we would have wrote to you long before this time. Myself Isaac and Lida are living here together   Emma is working out   She was at home last Sabbath. She is well we See her most every week   we got a letter not long Since from Martha   She has been very Sick ever Since the first of July until about three weeks ago   She was just So She could Sit up was So weak She could Scarcely write   the rest of the Friends ware well. now I will tell you Something about the health & the weather. we had a very hot Summer   one of the hotest I ever Saw   the fall has been rather cool   not much rain of late. this was the Sickliest fall we have had here for many years   a good many Deaths   the prevailing disease was the Flux.[44] I would like very much to visit Merom & your people if I had the means to do So but have not at present   I may be able to visit you Sometime. tell [*illegible deletion*] Willard if he lives he must come & See us Sometime. if nothing very unfavorable takes place there will be Something coming to him from us Some day   I am Still trying to live the life of a Christian & gain a home in heaven   I hope you will remember me at the throne of grace   Crops the last year ware good   wheat looks pretty well this fall   if you ever take a notion to travel be Shure to make us a visit   I will now bring my letter to a close hoping you will Soon reply

Your Father & Friend
John Walters[45]

NOTES

1. McPherson, *Battle Cry of Freedom*, 844–852.

2. Jordan, *Marching Home*, 152–158.

3. Pension file, David W. Walters, Pvt., Co. I, 5 Ind. Cav.; Civil War, RG 15; NA-Washington.

4. George W. Stalnaker testified that "when he first met said soldier in prison which was about the 15' day of August 1864, he was in good health, that in consequences of the hardships and short rations and want of attention, said soldier began gradually to fail and on or about the 15' day of January 1865 he became so weak and debilitated that he was unable longer to be up, his voice sank, could not speak louder than a whisper. There was nothing of him, appearantly, but 'skin and bones.' There was no medical attendance provide for him. There was no medicine given him by reason of which mistreatment he died as above stated. That he obtained knowledge of the above and foregiving facts in regard to said Soldier, by being himself in the service of the United States at the same time, as a private in Company 'K' Commanded by Captain George Julian, of the 99th Regiment of Ind. Volunteers, and being in the same Rebel prison at the same time with said David W. Walters, deceased, from about the 15' day of August 1864, until he died as above stated once being personally well acquainted with said Soldier before he entered the service He saw him and was with him almost every day until he died" (pension file, David W. Walters, Pvt., Co. I, 5 Ind. Cav.; Civil War, RG 15; NA-Washington).

5. Barton, *The Life of Clara Barton*, 316.

6. Terry Reimer (National Civil War Medicine Museum), interview with Lynn Heidelbaugh, October 22, 2019.

7. Official documents with reference to Rachel J. (Ward) Walters are preserved in the records of the men in the Walters and Ward families—Rachel's father, husband, and son. The date Willard Walters became eligible for the minor's pension was December 16, 1868, the day following his mother's death. This date is handwritten on Willard O. Walters's pension certificate for minor heir, date stamped 1873 (not transcribed, 1991.0291.136, National Postal Museum, Smithsonian Institution). Rachel's date of death in Sullivan County, Indiana, also appears in several forms for Willard's pension claims, including the January 8, 1870, Guardian's Declaration for Minor Children's Army Pension, pension file, David W. Walters, Pvt., Co. I, 5 Ind. Cav.; Civil War, RG 15; NA-Washington.

8. The exact number of children left orphaned is not known. James Marten explained, "Although comprehensive statistics on children entering orphanages and asylums due to the deaths of soldier-fathers are unavailable, anecdotal evidence suggest there were thousands of war orphans . . . as many orphan-

ages opened in the 1860s as in the two previous decades" (*The Children's Civil War*, 211).

9. Marten, *The Children's Civil War*, 212, 211–217.

10. The June 25, 1880, letter (1991.0291.137, National Postal Museum, Smithsonian Institution) sent by Samuel Wall, pension claims and collection specialist of Sullivan County, Indiana, was likely addressed to Willard O. Walters regarding the pension from David Walters's military service. A minor was eligible for a Civil War pension until the age of sixteen, which Willard reached on September 15, 1877. Wall's letter referred to a blank form that was to be completed by a guardian. This may be the unused pension form entitled Application of Children for Additional Bounty, Act, July 28, 1866 (1991.0291.138, National Postal Museum, Smithsonian Institution). The two documents are not transcribed.

11. The Twentieth Indiana was still in winter quarters near the trenches of Petersburg, Virginia, continuing the siege of the city.

12. The envelope (1991.0291.99) for this letter (1991.0291.98) was postmarked "WASHINGTON / D.C / JAN 18" over a three-cent George Washington stamp. It was addressed "Mrs. Rachel. J. Walters / Star City / Pulaski Co Ind." The letter was written on blue-lined paper.

13. The Twentieth Indiana participated in the Battle of Hatcher's Run, February 5–7, 1865, during the siege of Petersburg, Virginia, and continued to camp outside the city.

14. There is not a letter in the collection by David Walters from this time.

15. Indiana.

16. The envelope (1991.0291.101) for this letter (1991.0291.100) was postmarked "WASHINGTON / D.C / [*illegible*]" over a three-cent George Washington stamp. It was addressed "Mrs. Rachel. J. Walters / Star City / Pulaski Co / Ind." The letter was written on blue-lined stationery embossed with a paper manufacturer's mark.

17. After the Union forces broke the siege of Petersburg on April 2, the Twentieth Indiana participated in the pursuit of the Confederate army as it retreated westward. The regiment was most likely near Farmville, Virginia, while it waited for orders that Isaac describes in this letter.

18. Confederate general Robert E. Lee surrendered his Army of Northern Virginia to Union general Ulysses S. Grant at Appomattox Court House on April 9, 1865. This was not the last Confederate army to surrender; nevertheless, the capitulation of Lee was considered to be the beginning of the end of the war.

19. Although Secretary of State William H. Seward and his thirty-four-year-old son Frederick were attacked at home by the Lincoln assassination coconspirator Lewis Powell, only President Abraham Lincoln perished in the simultaneous attack at Ford's Theatre.

20. The envelope (1991.0291.103) for this letter (1991.0291.102) was post-marked "OLD POINT COMFORT / VA / APR 21" and has a cancelled three-cent George Washington stamp. It was addressed "Mrs. Rachel. J. Walters. / Star City / Pulaski Co / Ind." The letter was written on blue-lined stationery embossed with a paper manufacturer's mark.

21. *Washington City* was a period term used for Washington, DC.

22. Isaac Walters continues to express grief over the death of his brother David as he did in his April 17 letter.

23. Burke's Station, Virginia.

24. Isaac describes the Grand Review of the Armies, a large military parade through Washington, DC, which took place on May 23 and 24, 1865, to celebrate the victorious Union armies. Civilians lined the city's streets to cheer on the Union soldiers as they were reviewed by numerous generals and politicians, including President Andrew Johnson.

25. The envelope (1991.0291.105) for this letter (1991.0291.104) was post-marked "WASHINGTON / D.C. / M[AY] 21" and has a cancelled three-cent George Washington stamp. It was addressed "Mr. Rachel J Walters / Star City / Pulaski Co / Ind." The letter was written on blue-lined paper.

26. Although John Louderback did not describe the contents of the tin case, such vessels were commonly carried to protect personal items like letters.

27. The letter (1991.0291.109) was written on stationery embossed with a paper manufacturer's mark. A matching envelope has not been identified.

28. Rachel Walters had received notice of her husband, David's, death in the letter (1991.0291.109) dated May 27, 1865, from John S. Louderback; however, it was likely that the details were not sufficient for a pension application.

29. The postal markings on the envelope (1991.0291.63) for this letter (1991.0291.62) indicate that John Louderback did not receive it. The envelope is addressed "Capt John S Lounderback / Plymouth, Ind / (Marshal Co)." It has a cancelled three-cent George Washington stamp on the right and is postmarked "WINAMAC / IND / APR 27," below which is stamped "ADV / MAY 30 / 186[*blank space*]" to signify that it was "advertised" for Louderback to pick up the letter at the Plymouth, Indiana, post office. On the envelope's back, a postal employee wrote "Not called for" and stamped it "PLYMOUTH / IND / [*illegible*]." Another envelope (1991.0291.161) in the collection carried this mail back to Rachel Walters. It was from the Post Office Department Return Letter Office with a partial marking "[MIS]SENT / [JU]L 23 / [186]6" and was addressed "Mrs. Rachel J. Walters / P.O. Box 107 / Winamac / Ind."

30. The letter was signed by a proxy for Clara Barton as indicated by "per@," an abbreviation for *per procurationem*. The envelope (1991.0291.132) for this letter (1991.0291.131) was addressed "Mrs. Rachel J. Walters / Winamac / Ind," is post-marked "WASHINGTON D.C. / JUL 12 / FREE," and bears the free frank "H

Wilson." Henry Wilson served as US senator from Massachusetts (1855–1873), supported Clara Barton's wartime work, and championed the Missing Soldiers Office, including extending his franking privilege to the mail from this office.

31. Rachel Walters was referring to the letter (1991.0291.131) from the Missing Soldiers Office sent on July 12, 1866.

32. A message was written on the back of this letter (1991.0291.64) by a worker in the Missing Soldiers Office, and the letter was returned to Rachel Walters. The response was signed by a proxy for Clara Barton as indicated by *pera*, an abbreviation for *per procurationem*. A matching envelope has not been identified.

33. Ai, Fulton County, Ohio.

34. The writers, presumed to be Emmaline "Emma" Walters and Martha "Mattie" Walters, sisters-in-law of Rachel Walters, did not sign their last names. According to the 1870 Census, their father, John Walters, was living in the household of their brother Isaac in Ai, Ohio, but Emmaline and Martha were not listed for that household (1870 U.S. Census, Fulton, Fulton County, Ohio, page 103B, dwelling 161, family 162, Isaac Walters; digital image, Ancestry.com, accessed May 11, 2021).

35. This may refer to Rachel J. (Ward) Walters's sister Phebe A. (Ward) Dunkin, who married William H. Johnston on July 4, 1866.

36. Fort Wayne, Indiana.

37. The envelope (1991.0291.111) for this letter (1991.0291.110) has a three-cent George Washington stamp with handwritten cancellation "Ai O Ag /66." It was addressed "Mrs Rachel. J. Walters / Winamac / Pulaski Co, / Indiana." The letter was written on stationery embossed with a shield.

38. Private George McKinsey, of Valparaiso, Indiana, served in Company I of the Fifth Indiana Cavalry alongside David Walters and John Louderback.

39. The envelope (1991.0291.113) for this letter (1991.0291.112) has a cancelled three-cent George Washington stamp and is postmarked "[VAL]PARAISO. JAN / 1867" in the upper left corner. It was addressed "When / Miss / Rachel Walters / Star City / Ind." The letter was written on blue-lined stationery embossed with a paper manufacturer's mark.

40. Russell P. Finney, of Richmond, Indiana, served in Company H of the Fifth Indiana Cavalry from August to December 1862, when he was promoted to captain of Company M. He transferred to the Sixth Indiana Cavalry in March 1864 and rose to the rank of major (compiled military service record, Russel P. Finney, Maj., Co. H and M, 5 Ind. Cav, Co. B, 6 Ind. Cav., RG 94; NA-Washington).

41. Although a matching envelope has not been identified, Rachel Walters received Russell P. Finney's letter (1991.0291.133) sent by a staff member of the Missing Soldiers Office with a notation added to the back of the sheet and signed twice in the name of "Clara Barton."

42. John Brown from Crown Point, Indiana, served in Company I of the Fifth Indiana Cavalry and was mustered out on June 15, 1865, as a sergeant (compiled military service record, John Brown, Sgt., Co. I, 5 Ind. Cav., RG 94; NA-Washington).

43. The letter was signed by a proxy for Clara Barton as indicated by the abbreviation for *per procurationem*. The envelope (1991.0291.135) for this letter (1991.0291.134) was addressed "Rachel. J. Walters / Winamac / Ind," was postmarked "WASHINGTON D.C. / OCT 16 / FREE," and bears the free franking signature, "H Wilson," of US senator Henry Wilson from Massachusetts (1855–1873), who supported Clara Barton's Missing Soldiers Office.

44. *Flux* was a period term for dysentery.

45. The 1870 federal census indicates that John Walters could not write, but he was able to read. At the time he was described as a retired farmer living in the household of his son Isaac, a farmer, and daughter-in-law Eliza (Terrell) Walters, along with Carrie Walters, age one, and Ida Terrell, age eight, in Fulton County, Ohio (1870 U.S. Census, Fulton, Fulton County, Ohio, page 103B, dwelling 161, family 162, Isaac Walters; digital image, Ancestry.com, accessed May 11, 2021). The envelope (1991.0291.128) for this letter (1991.0291.127) was postmarked "[S]WANTON / O. / OCT [*illegible*]" to the left of a cancelled three-cent George Washington stamp. It was addressed "Mrs Rachel Walters / Merom Sullivan / Co Ind." The letter was written in ink on stationery embossed with a paper manufacturer's mark.

—◆◆◆—

EPILOGUE

I am happy to Say to you to day that my life & health is Spared to
See the close of this cruel war which has brought So many of
the braver Sons of the North to their graves.

　　　　—Isaac Walters to his sister-in-law Rachel J. Walters, April 17, 1865

ISAAC WALTERS MUSTERED OUT AS a private on July 12, 1865, in Jeffer-
sonville, Indiana.[1] In 1867, he married Eliza Terrell, and a few years later, they
were living and farming in Ohio with one daughter.[2] He was admitted in 1897
to the National Home for Disabled Volunteer Soldiers, Marion, Grant County,
Indiana. His records from the Marion Branch show he was in and out of homes
throughout 1911 and that he suffered heart disease and chronic rheumatism,
contracted in July 1863 at Gettysburg, Pennsylvania, the site of one of the many
battles in which Isaac Walters had fought but one of the few not described in his
letters in this collection.[3] He died in Ohio in 1917.

John S. Louderback also lived through the war, and three of his letters to
Rachel Walters survive in this collection with pivotal information about her
husband, David. Their friendship dates to Walters's enlistment in 1862. Several
of David Walters's messages include references to Louderback—some of David's
even show similarities to Louderback's handwriting, and perhaps Louderback
gave David assistance with writing them. David also may have entrusted Louderback with carrying items home for him on at least one occasion.[4] Louderback
earned respect within the regiment and rose up the ranks from private to sergeant and received promotions to first lieutenant on July 1, 1864, and captain
on October 1, 1864. When taken as a prisoner of war following the company's
surrender in Stoneman's Raid near Macon, Georgia, in the last days of July 1864,

Willard and Amelia Walters, 1884. *(Courtesy of Emily Duffelmeyer)*

Louderback purportedly chose to remain with the enlisted men and endured the infamous Andersonville Prison. Following a transfer to Charleston, South Carolina, in October, he eventually arrived at the same POW camp in Florence, South Carolina, where David Walters would die in February 1865. Louderback and the POWs obtained their release in the spring, and he rejoined Company I, Fifth Indiana Cavalry, to muster out in June. By August 1865, Louderback moved from Fulton to Valparaiso, Indiana, where he established a grocery business and died in 1914 at age eighty.[5]

Willard O. Walters, orphaned at age seven by the passing of his mother, Rachel, and father, David, grew up in the care of his maternal grandparents, Samuel and Sarah Ward.[6] At age eighteen, he was working as a farm laborer and living with his grandmother and two uncles in Sullivan County, Indiana.[7] In 1884, he married Amelia M. Walter (born in Hillsdale, Michigan, on January 1, 1865). The couple's first child, Edna, was born in Missouri in 1885, followed by Arthur W., Winnie T., Victor S., Paul E., and Lauretta. By the time of the 1900 census, the family lived in Lamar, Barton County, Missouri, where Willard worked as jailor for the county.[8] Members of the Walters family began to work for the Post Office Department shortly after the first Rural Free Delivery service route was established in the township in August 1901.[9] The 1903 *Official Register of the United States*, which listed the names and job titles of all federal employees, included Arthur as a rural mail carrier and his mother, Amelia, as a substitute carrier.[10] Willard started his postal employment on June 1, 1906, on Rural Free Delivery route number 7 out of the Lamar post office, and his son Paul served as a substitute carrier from 1911 to 1921.[11] The four Walterses were, in a sense, following in the footsteps of Willard's grandfather, Samuel Ward Jr., who had been postmaster in Mooresburg, Indiana.[12] Willard worked for over two decades as a rural mail carrier, retiring in the year before his death on October 20, 1931. His family's letters passed down to his son Arthur Walters and granddaughter June (Walters) Leonard, who donated the collection to the Smithsonian Institution.

NOTES

1. Isaac Walters's brothers John Wesley and David both died during the war, but his elder brother Eli lived. Eli received a discharge after four months of service in 1862, returned home to his wife, resumed farming, and died in 1896 (1870 US Census, Royal Center, Cass County, Indiana, page 41B, dwelling 55, family 58, Eli Walters, digital image, Ancestry.com, accessed June 5, 2020; Huffman, "Genealogy Report: Descendants of Mathew Terrell").

2. 1870 US Census, Fulton, Fulton County, Ohio, page 103B, dwelling 161, family 162, Isaac Walters; digital image, Ancestry.com, accessed May 11, 2021.

3. US National Homes for Disabled Volunteer Soldiers, 1866–1938, Isaac Walters, Pvt., Co. F, 20 Ind. Inf.; Civil War, RG 15; NA-Washington.

4. David W. Walters to Rachel J. Walters, September 29, 1862, National Postal Museum, Smithsonian Institution, 1991.0291.5.

5. Goodspeed Brothers, *Pictorial and Biographical Record*, 150–151.

6. Pension file, David W. Walters, Pvt., Co. I, 5 Ind. Cav.; Civil War, RG 15; NA-Washington.

7. 1880 US Census, Gill, Sullivan County, Indiana, page 629B, dwelling 84, family 85, Willard O. Walters, digital image, Ancestry.com, accessed June 5, 2020.

8. 1900 US Census, Lamar, Barton County, Missouri, page 24, dwelling 506, family 508, Willard O. Walters, digital image, Ancestry.com, accessed June 5, 2020.

9. Historian of United States Postal Service, "Missouri: Dates That First Rural Routes Were Established at Post Offices, Through 1904."

10. United States Bureau of the Census, *Official Register of the United States ... 1903*, 1223. Arthur W. Walters continued to work for the Post Office Department in Missouri and Idaho before retiring in California (Accession file 0.256400, National Postal Museum, Smithsonian Institution, Washington, DC).

11. Official personnel folder, Willard O. Walters, rural carrier, Lamar Office, Barton County, Missouri; NA-St. Louis.

12. Samuel Ward Jr. was the postmaster of Mooresburg, Harrison Township, Pulaski County, Indiana, from June 2, 1853, to July 28, 1862, when the post office was discontinued (Goodspeed and Battey, *Counties of White and Pulaski, Indiana*, 555; United States Department of State, *Official Register ... 1853*, 482; United States Department of Interior, *Official Register ... 1863*, 366).

AFTERWORD

I hope these lines will find you as well as they leave me pray for me
dear David that I may live more in the discharge of my duty that I
may trust you to his kind care and protection while in the enemies
land and that he may grant you a safe and speedy return

—Rachel Walters to her husband, David, June 2, 186[4]

OUR RESEARCH LED US TO a myriad of subjects and source material. We
returned to two subjects over and over to seek additional information: photographs of the Walters family and the death of David Walters. We hope someday
that a new search for the whereabouts of photographs will locate images of
the Walters and Ward families from the Civil War period. There are numerous
mentions of photographs throughout the letters. Most Americans could afford
tintypes and cartes-de-viste, and they readily exchanged their images with one
another during the war. Photographers often set up studios in cities, and many
soldiers and families back home invested in having a photograph taken to help
ameliorate the separation they faced. Some photographers even traveled into
the field and took pictures of soldiers in camps or on battlefields. Isaac, David,
and Rachel Walters all specifically described pictures made of themselves and
of young Willard Walters. They frequently commented on their looks and requested photographs. Yet, despite the written evidence that photographs of the
Walterses were taken during the war, none of these images could be located
during the research for this publication. The Walters descendants June Leonard,
Cynthia Crank, and Emily Duffelmeyer generously offered assistance with images of Willard Walters in adulthood. Contacting local historical societies and
archives did not yield images, except for a few identified and many unidentified

members of regiments in which the Walterses were enrolled. Through consulta-
tions with experts at the Center for Civil War Photography and *Military Images*
magazine, we learned that most images taken during the war were generally
meant for immediate family members and were not typically labeled.[1] The subjects in many of the surviving photos are unnamed.

Still, the most difficult challenge we faced while researching the letters of the
Walters family was determining the final fate of David Walters. Although John
S. Louderback's May 27, 1865, letter claimed that David Walters died of malnutrition as a result of conditions in a prisoner-of-war camp, other evidence suggests
he died as a result of wounds received at the Battle of Resaca. The inconsistencies
of the testimony in the letters and other wartime documents highlight some of
the challenges of historical sources.

According to an entry in the US National Cemeteries Register, David W.
Walters, of Company I, Fifth Indiana Cavalry, died on June 5, 1864, and was
originally buried near Kingston, Georgia.[2] The burial records indicate that David Walters was wounded and captured on May 14, 1864, at the Battle of Resaca,
which took place about thirty miles north of Kingston. It is possible that David
could have been wounded at the battle and succumbed to those wounds on
June 5. The remains at Kingston, Georgia, were later reinterred in grave A-473
of the Marietta National Cemetery in Canton, Georgia, where a headstone in
the name of David Walters still stands.

The June 5, 1864, death date is contradicted multiple times within the letters
of the collection. On May 22, 1864, John S. Louderback sent news to Rachel
Walters that her husband, David, had been captured a few days prior at the
Battle of Resaca. Louderback wrote to Rachel just over a year later, on May 27,
1865, with news of David's death at the prisoner-of-war camp in Florence, South
Carolina, in February 1865. He explained that he last saw David in the prison
about the fifth of the month and was told by reliable sources that David died
about the tenth.

Rachel also received letters from her brother-in-law Isaac Walters that seem
to disprove that David died in June 1864. Isaac Walters wrote to Rachel on
December 19, 1864, and February 19, 1865, of word that had been received from
David Walters. In his December letter, Isaac recounted, "I was overjoyed to hear
from David feel thankful that his life has been Spared So far & hope he may have
a Speedey return home to his Anxious Companion & Friends I hope I may be
So happy as to as to meet him once more on Earth & while we yet are Soldiers."
In February, Isaac mentioned hearing again from David, stating, "[A]m glad to
hear from David. it is not only a great consolation to you but all his Friends. I
hope his life may be Spared to return home to his Friends & we may be permitted to enjoy each others Company many long days that are yet in the Future I

often think of him & wonder how he is getting along to day or to night & where he is, what he has to eat & to wear how he is treated & my heart cries for our poor unfortunate prisoners." Such letters from David during his time in prison do not exist in the collection. Isaac's statements, however, seem to disprove that David could have died in June 1864.

One letter that Rachel received from Clara Barton's Missing Soldiers Office while she was gathering documentation for a pension application testifies to David being unaccounted for after the Battle of Resaca. The office staff forwarded the letter received from Russell P. Finney written on February 27, 1867. Finney served with the Fifth Indiana Cavalry and David at the time of the Battle of Resaca. He wrote of David, "Evidently Killed by the enemy at Resaca, Ga. on 14th day of May 1864," and further explained how he saw David before he was captured and that others "report that Walters, was never heard of after the fight." An alternative account came through the Missing Soldiers Office, sent by John Brown, a veteran of the Fifth Indiana Cavalry, with the testimony that David Walters "died at Florence S.C. Februay 25th 1865." Other documents assembled by Rachel in order to receive a pension also described David dying while a prisoner in Florence, South Carolina.[3] The date, location, and cause of David Walters's death are officially described in records of Willard Walters's claim for a minor's pension: "Credible witness testifies that the soldier died in Rebel prison at Florence S.C. Feb 28 1865 of bad treatment."[4] It is this date and location that appear on the family tree and map in this publication.

In a time before dog tags and DNA analysis, misidentification of lost soldiers was a common occurrence. The identification of lost comrades depended on living members of their unit who could identify the remains. Thousands of graves throughout cemeteries from the Civil War are simply marked "unknown."

We may never know with certainty the fate of David Walters. What we do know, however, is that he represents one of the over six hundred thousand young men who left their homes and families, suffered through great hardship, and never returned to see those they loved. Although a grave exists for him in Georgia, it is unlikely to contain his remains. David Walters most likely rests outside the former prisoner-of-war camp in Florence, South Carolina, as "an American soldier known but to God."

NOTES

1. Bob Zeller (Center for Civil War Photography), email to Thomas J. Paone, January 30, 2020; Ronald S. Coddington and Rick Brown (*Military Images*), emails to Thomas J. Paone, January 31, 2020, and February 16, 2020.

2. US, Burial Registers, Military Posts and National Cemeteries, 1862–1960, Ancestry.com.

3. John S. Louderback to Rachel J. Walters, May 27, 1865 (1991.0291.109); John S. Louderback to Rachel J. Walters, January 17, 1867 (1991.0291.112); pension file, David W. Walters, Pvt., Co. I, 5 Ind. Cav.; Civil War, RG 15; NA-Washington.

4. Pension file, David W. Walters, Pvt., Co. I, 5 Ind. Cav.; Civil War, RG 15; NA-Washington.

BIBLIOGRAPHY

Accession file 0.256400, National Postal Museum, Smithsonian Institution, Washington, DC.

Accession file 1991.0291, National Postal Museum, Smithsonian Institution, Washington, DC.

Attie, Jeanie. "Warwork and the Crisis of Domesticity in the North." In *Divided Houses: Gender and Civil War*, edited by Elizabeth Clinton and Nina Silber, 247–259. New York: Oxford University Press, 1993.

Bailey, Lucy. "'So Pleasant to Be a School Maam': The Civil War as an Educational Force for Women." *Advancing Women in Leadership Journal* 29, no. 11 (2009), http://advancingwomen.com/awl/awl_wordpress/.

Baker, J. David. *The Postal History of Indiana*. Louisville, KY: L. H. Hartmann, 1976.

Ballard, Michael B. *Vicksburg: The Campaign That Opened the Mississippi*. Chapel Hill: University of North Carolina Press, 2004.

Barnhart, John D. "The Impact of the Civil War on Indiana." *Indiana Magazine of History* 57, no. 3 (September 1961): 185–224.

Barton, William. *The Life of Clara Barton: Founder of the American Red Cross*. Vol. 1. Boston: Houghton, Mifflin, 1922.

Benton, Josiah H. *Voting in the Field: A Forgotten Chapter of the Civil War*. Boston: Plimpton Press, 1915.

Billings, John D. *Hardtack and Coffee: The Unwritten Story of Army Life*. Lincoln: University of Nebraska Press, 1993.

Blevins, Cameron. *Paper Trails: The U.S. Post and the Making of the American West*. New York: Oxford University Press, 2021.

Bohannon, Keith S. "Disgraced and Ruined by the Decision of the Court: The Court-Martial of Emory F. Best, C.S.A." In *Chancellorsville: The Battle and*

Its Aftermath, edited by Gary W. Gallagher, 200–218. Chapel Hill: University of North Carolina Press, 1996.

Bui, Long Bao. "'I Feel Impelled to Write': Male Intimacy, Epistolary Privacy, and the Culture of Letter Writing during the American Civil War." PhD diss., University of Illinois at Urbana-Champaign, 2016.

Campion, Thomas J. "Indian Removal and the Transformation of Northern Indiana." *Indiana Magazine of History* 107, no. 1 (2011): 32–62.

Carter, Russ W. *War Ballots: Military Voting by Mail from the Civil War to WWII.* Cypress, TX: Military Postal History Society, 2005.

Charles, Harry K. "American Civil War Postage Due: North and South." American Philatelic Society. Accessed April 29, 2020. https://stamps.org/Portals /o/Symposium/CharlesPaper.pdf.

Chronicling America: Historic American Newspapers. Library of Congress. "'Martial Law in Kentucky,' *The Nashville Daily Union.* (Nashville, TN) 1862–1866, August 02, 1863, Image 2." Accessed May 31, 2020. https:// chroniclingamerica.loc.gov/lccn/sn83025718/1863-08-02/ed-1/seq-2/.

Cimprich, John. *Fort Pillow: A Civil War Massacre, and Public Memory.* Baton Rouge: Louisiana State University Press, 2011.

Civil War and Later Pension Files. Record Group 15: Department of Veterans Affairs. National Archives, Washington, DC.

Civilian Personnel Files. Post Office Department 1919–1951. National Archives, St. Louis, MO.

Clifford, Geraldine Jonçich. *Those Good Gertrudes: A Social History of Women Teachers in America.* Baltimore, MD: Johns Hopkins University Press, 2014.

Dixon, Ina. "Modern Medicine's Civil War Legacy." American Battlefield Trust. Accessed May 11, 2020. https://www.battlefields.org/learn/articles/civil-war -medicine.

Etcheson, Nicole. "Women and the Family at Home in the North." In *Women and the American Civil War: North-South Counterpoints*, edited by Judith Giesberg and Randall M. Miller, 190–211. Kent, OH: Kent State Press, 2018.

Faust, Drew Gilpin. "'The Dread Void of Uncertainty': Naming the Dead in the American Civil War." *Southern Cultures* 11, no. 2 (Summer 2005): 7–32.

Faust, Drew Gilpin. *This Republic of Suffering: Death and the American Civil War.* New York: Alfred A. Knopf, 2012.

Fuller, A. James. *Oliver P. Morton and the Politics of the Civil War and Reconstruction.* Kent, OH: Kent State University Press, 2017.

Furlough and Certificate of Disability, David W. Walters. Catalog Number M-11136. Division of Medicine and Science, National Museum of American History, Smithsonian Institution, Washington, DC.

Gallagher, Gary W. *Chancellorsville: The Battle and Its Aftermath.* Chapel Hill: University of North Carolina Press, 1996.

Gallagher, Gary W. *The Union War*. Cambridge, MA: Harvard University Press, 2011.

Giesberg, Judith. *Army at Home: Women and the Civil War on the Northern Home Front*. Chapel Hill: University of North Carolina Press, 2009.

Gilbreath, Erasmus Corwin, and Susan Gilbreath Lane. *Dignity of Duty: The Journals of Erasmus Corwin Gilbreath, 1861–1898: A Personal Odyssey of Service from the Civil War to the Spanish-American War*. Chicago: Pritzker Military Museum and Library, 2015.

Gill, Diana C. *How We Are Changed by War: A Study of Letters and Diaries from Colonial Conflicts to Operation Iraqi Freedom*. New York: Routledge, 2010.

Glatthaar, Joseph T. *The March to the Sea and Beyond: Sherman's Troops in the Savannah and Carolinas Campaign*. Baton Rouge: Louisiana State University Press, 1995.

Goodspeed Brothers. *Pictorial and Biographical Record of La Porte, Porter, Lake and Starke Counties, Indiana: Containing Biographical and Genealogical Records of Leading Men, Women and Prominent Families of the Counties Named, and of Other Portions of the State*. Chicago: Goodspeed Bros, 1894.

Goodspeed, Weston Arthur, and F. A. Battey. *Counties of White and Pulaski, Indiana: Historical and Biographical*. Chicago: F. A. Battey, 1883.

Gordon, Leon M. "The Price of Isolation in Northern Indiana, 1830–1860." *Indiana Magazine of History* 46, no. 2 (1950): 151–64.

Graham, Richard B. "Mail for the Army." *S.P.A. Journal* 26, no. 5 (January 1964): 325–331.

Graham, Richard B. "Soldier's Letters." *S.P.A. Journal* 25, no. 10 (June 1963): 555–559.

Guelzo, Allen C. *Gettysburg: The Last Invasion*. New York: Alfred A. Knopf, 2013.

Hager, Christopher. *"I Remain Yours": Common Lives in Civil War Letters*. Cambridge, MA: Harvard University Press, 2018.

Henkin, David M. *The Postal Age: The Emergence of Modern Communications in Nineteenth-Century America*. Chicago: University of Chicago Press, 2007.

Hess, Earl J. *The Union Soldier in Battle: Enduring the Ordeal of Combat*. Lawrence: University of Kansas Press, 1997.

Hinman, Wilbur F. *Corporal Si Klegg and His "Pard": How They Lived and Talked and What They Did and Suffered while Fighting for the Flag*. 10th ed. Cleveland, OH: N. G. Hamilton, 1895.

Historian of United States Postal Service. "Missouri: Dates That First Rural Routes Were Established at Post Offices, through 1904." April 2008. https://about.usps.com/who-we-are/postal-history/first-rural-routes.htm.

Historical Register of National Homes for Disabled Volunteer Soldiers, 1866–1938. National Archives Microfilm Publication M1749, 282 rolls. Records of the Department of Veterans Affairs, Record Group 15. National Archives, Washington, DC.

Huffman, Jeannine. "Genealogy Report: Descendants of Mathew Terrell." Accessed April 6, 2015. https://www.genealogy.com/ftm/h/u/f/Jeannine -Huffman/GENE9-0004.html.

Indiana. Cass County. 1860 US Census. Digital images. Ancestry.com. Accessed May 17, 2021. http://ancestry.com.

Indiana. Cass County. 1870 US Census. Digital images. Ancestry.com. Accessed June 5, 2020. http://ancestry.com.

Indiana. Pulaski County. 1850 US Census. Digital images. Ancestry.com. Accessed May 11, 2021. http://ancestry.com.

Indiana. Pulaski County. 1860 US Census. Digital images. Ancestry.com. Accessed May 11, 2021. http://ancestry.com.

Indiana. Sullivan County. 1880 US Census. Digital images. Ancestry.com. Accessed June 5, 2020. http://ancestry.com.

Indiana and William Henry Harrison Terrell. *Report of the Adjutant General of the State of Indiana.* Vol. 4. Indianapolis: A. H. Connor State Printer, 1865.

Indiana Digital Archives. "Military Records, Joseph Walters." Accessed May 11, 2020. http://secure.in.gov/apps/iara/search/Home/Detail?rId=1044437.

Indiana Infantry. *History of the Forty-Sixth Regiment Indiana Volunteer Infantry: September,1861–September,1865.* Logansport, IN: Wilson, Humphreys, 1888.

Jordan, Brian Matthew. *Marching Home: Union Veterans and Their Unending Civil War.* New York: Liveright, 2014.

Ledoux, Albert H. *The Florence Stockade: A Chronicle of Prison Life in the Waning Months of the Civil War.* Gallitzin, PA: Albert H. Ledoux, 2015.

Ledoux, Albert H. *The Union Dead of the Florence Stockade.* Hartsville: Old Darlington District Chapter, South Carolina Genealogical Society, 2000.

Lord, Francis A. *Civil War Sutlers and Their Wares.* New York: T. Yoseloff, 1969.

Marten, James A. *The Children's Civil War.* Chapel Hill: University of North Carolina Press, 1998.

McPherson, James. *Battle Cry of Freedom.* New York: Oxford University Press, 1988.

McPherson, James. *For Cause and Comrades: Why Men Fought in the Civil War.* New York: Oxford University Press, 1997.

McPherson, James. *War on the Waters: The Union and Confederate Navies, 1861– 1865.* Chapel Hill: University of North Carolina Press, 2012.

Military, Compiled Service Records. Civil War. Carded Records, Volunteer Organizations. Records of the Adjutant General's Office, 1890–1912, Record Group 94. National Archives, Washington, DC.

"Milton V. Sellers in the Indiana, Marriage Index, 1800–1941." Ancestry.com. Accessed May 11, 2020. http://ancestry.com.

Missouri. Barton County. 1900 US Census. Digital images. Ancestry.com. Accessed June 5, 2020. http://ancestry.com.

Nation, Richard Franklin, and Stephen E. Towne. *Indiana's War: The Civil War in Documents.* Athens: Ohio University Press, 2009.

National Park Service. "Battle Unit Details, Union Indiana Volunteers, 5th Regiment, Indiana Cavalry (90th Regiment, Indiana Volunteers)." Accessed May 11, 2020. https://www.nps.gov/civilwar/search-battle-units-detail.htm ?battleUnitCode=UIN0005RC.

National Park Service. "Battle Unit Details, Union Indiana Volunteers, 20th Regiment, Indiana Infantry." Accessed May 11, 2020. https://www.nps.gov /civilwar/search-battle-units-detail.htm?battleUnitCode=UIN0020RI.

National Park Service. "Battle Unit Details, Union Indiana Volunteers, 46th Regiment, Indiana Infantry." Accessed May 11, 2020. https://www.nps.gov /civilwar/search-battle-units-detail.htm?battleUnitCode=UIN0046RI.

National Park Service. "Morgan's Raid in Kentucky, Indiana and Ohio, National Register of Historic Places Continuation Sheet." July 19, 2016. https:// www.nps.gov/nr/feature/places/pdfs/64501229.pdf.

Nelson, Michael C. "Writing during Wartime: Gender and Literacy in the American Civil War." *Journal of American Studies* 31, no. 1 (1997): 43–68.

Ohio. Fulton County. 1870 US Census. Digital images. Ancestry.com. Accessed May 11, 2021. http://ancestry.com.

Parker, David B., and Torrance Parker. *A Chautauqua Boy in '61 and Afterward; Reminiscences by David B. Parker, Second Lieutenant, Seventy-Second New York, Detailed Superintendent of the Mails of the Army of the Potomac, United States Marshal, District of Virginia, Chief Post Office Inspector.* Boston: Small, Maynard, 1912.

Perlmann, Joel, and Robert A. Margo. *Women's Work?: American Schoolteachers, 1650–1920.* Chicago: University of Chicago Press, 2001.

Rable, George C. *God's Almost Chosen Peoples: A Religious History of the American Civil War.* Chapel Hill: University of North Carolina Press, 2015.

Rhoades, Nancy L., and Lucy E. Bailey. *Wanted—Correspondence: Women's Letters to a Union Soldier.* Athens: Ohio University Press, 2009.

Rodgers, Thomas E. "Hoosier Women and the Civil War Home Front." *Indiana Magazine of History* 97, no. 2 (June 2001): 105–128.

Rosiecki, Casimer. "Gettysburg in My Hometown: Lieut. Col. Taylor, 20th Indiana Infantry." The Blog of Gettysburg National Military Park. Last modified September 18, 2014. https://npsgnmp.wordpress.com/2014/09/18 /gettysburg-in-my-hometown-lieut-col-taylor-20th-indiana-infantry/.

Scheele, Carl H. *A Short History of the Mail Service.* Washington, DC: Smithsonian Institution Press, 1977.

Scott, Gary. "Clara Barton's: Civil War Apartments." *Washington History* 13, no. 1 (Spring/Summer 2001): 24–31.

Sears, Stephen W. *To the Gates of Richmond: The Peninsula Campaign*. New York: Ticknor and Fields, 1992.

Trudeau, Noah Andre. *The Last Citadel: Petersburg, Virginia June 1864–April 1865*. Baton Rouge: Louisiana State University Press, 1991.

United States Bureau of the Census. *Official Register of the United States . . . 1903, v.2*. Washington, DC: US Government Printing Office, 1903.

United States Department of Interior. *Official Register of the United States . . . 1863*. Washington, DC: US Government Printing Office, 1864.

United States Department of State. *Official Register of the United States . . . 1853*. Washington, DC: Robert Armstrong Public Printer, 1853.

United States Post Office Department. *Annual Reports of the Post Office Department for the Fiscal Year Ended June 30, 1898, Report of the Postmaster-General, Miscellaneous Reports*. Washington, DC: US Government Printing Office, 1898.

United States Post Office Department. *Postal Laws and Regulations of the United States of America, Published in Accordance with the Act of Congress, Approved March 3, 1879*. Washington, DC: US Government Printing Office, 1879.

United States Postal Service. *The United States Postal Service: An American History*. Washington, DC: US Postal Service, 2020. https://about.usps.com /publications/pub100.pdf.

"U.S., Burial Registers, Military Posts and National Cemeteries, 1862–1960," Digital Image s.v. "D W Walters." Ancestry.com. Accessed June 5, 2020. http://ancestry.com.

Weber, Jennifer L. *Copperheads: The Rise and Fall of Lincoln's Opponents in the North*. New York: Oxford University Press, 2008.

Weidman, Budge. "'Dear Husband, Please Come Home,' Civil War Letters to Black Soldiers." *Prologue: The Journal of the National Archives* 35, no. 4 (Winter 2004): 60–67.

Wheeler, Tom. *Mr. Lincoln's T-Mails: The Untold Story of How Abraham Lincoln Used the Telegraph to Win the Civil War*. New York: Collins, 2006.

Whites, LeeAnn. "The Civil War as a Crisis in Gender." In *Divided Houses: Gender and Civil War*, edited by Elizabeth Clinton and Nina Silber, 3–21. New York: Oxford University Press, 1993.

Whites, LeeAnn. "Written on the Heart: Soldiers' Letters, the Household Supply Line, and the Relational War." In *Household War: How Americans Lived and Fought the Civil War*, edited by Lisa Tendrich Frank and LeeAnn Whites, 118–134. Athens: University of Georgia Press, 2020.

Zeller, Bob. *The Blue and Gray in Black and White: A History of Civil War Photography*. Westport, CT: Praeger, 2005.

INDEX

Italic numerals indicate illustrations.

LYNN HEIDELBAUGH, curator at the Smithsonian National Postal Museum, specializes in the history of the US Postal Service. Heidelbaugh has published essays and created several exhibitions about military mail, including "Letters Home" in *Smithsonian Civil War: Inside the National Collection* and the exhibition *My Fellow Soldiers: Letter from World War I*, for which she received a Smithsonian Secretary's Award for Research. ORCID iD: 0000-0001-5097-9788.

THOMAS J. PAONE curates the lighter-than-air collection, including balloons, blimps, and airships, at the Smithsonian National Air and Space Museum. Paone's research focuses on ballooning in the Civil War as well as the use of airships and blimps in America. He is coauthor of *Milestones of Flight: The Epic of Aviation with the National Air and Space Museum*. ORCID iD: 0000-0002-5411-7007.

www.ingramcontent.com/pod-product-compliance
Lightning Source LLC
Chambersburg PA
CBHW050342030726
47503CB00008B/2574